150 YEARS OF ARTISTS' LITHOGRAPHS

Also by Felix H. Man

EIGHT EUROPEAN ARTISTS

★

Bey d. G. Zeller in München.

Nach der Natur auf Stein gezeichnet von Lorenz Quaglio 1818.

Aloys Senefelder

Erfinder der Lithographie und der chemischen Druckerey.

FELIX H. MAN

150 YEARS OF
ARTISTS'
LITHOGRAPHS

1803 - 1953

WILLIAM HEINEMANN LTD · LONDON · MELBOURNE · TORONTO

First published 1953

Printed by W. S. Cowell Ltd, at the Butter Market, Ipswich, England

Contents

INTRODUCTION BY JAMES LAVER

Nothing differentiates the human animal more sharply from the rest of organic life than his desire and ability to draw. Sometime in the remote past—how remote we are only just beginning to realise—this border-line was crossed: the eye not only saw, but perceived and remembered, the human mind toyed with an image, and the human hand sought means to set it down.

The ideograph, which seems to us more primitive than the literal transcription, contains so much of mind that we should hesitate to give it historical priority. For what a complicated thinking machine primitive man must have become before he was able, inside a cave, to imagine the buffalo he had seen outside, and with the simple means at his disposal to recreate it on a wall of rock! And to recreate not merely its shape but its action, and to incorporate into his picture something of his own desire!

There are scratchings on bone and ivory, markings, no doubt, on bark and leather, long perished, but the early artist's only "big canvas" was a rock-face, and some of the very earliest drawings must have been lithographs—drawings on stone. Later, as his technology advanced, man found other materials, potsherds and wooden panels, canvas, parchment and paper, and when he did use stone it was no longer the natural wall of the cavern but the artificial wall of the temple or church. Then, at the end of the Middle Ages, he forgot about stone altogether. For now he was more restless than his forebears. He wished to travel to and fro, to transport himself from place to place, and to take his works of art with him.

And with this new restlessness, which is perhaps what we mean by the Renaissance, a new desire began to spring up in his mind. He wished not only to create a work of art but to multiply it; and so there came into existence the holy pictures, the playing cards, the block-books engraved on wood and multiplied by successive impressions. What had stone to do with such an enterprise? Wood could be used, and metal also. The goldsmiths discovered that they could fill the channels cut by their gravers with ink, press paper against them, and obtain copies of their patterns. The armourers found out that their etched lines could be used in the same way. The rival techniques of engraving and etching were discovered together and with relief printing from wood-blocks maintained their place for three whole centuries as the only reproductive arts.

Their triumphs need no stressing. Engravings and etchings form the bulk of the treasured material in the great Print Rooms of the world and in private collections. The engravings of Dürer, the etchings of Rembrandt: in these two names the processes attained their peak of achievement. The third great process, that of wood-engraving, never quite reached the same heights. The wood-engravings of Dürer are splendid things, but how much had Dürer to do with them? Not very much, according to the scholars. His participation was limited to making a drawing for the *Formschneider* who cut the block, and no doubt, to overseeing and correcting the final result. But what we see is at best a translation. It lacks the impress of the Master's hand.

With his engravings, of course, we are on surer ground. In this medium Dürer himself was a most accomplished craftsman, but even here he had to *translate* the chiaroscuro of his original drawing into the curved lines and cross-hatching of trenches cut into a sheet of copper. Later, when the man who made the drawing and the man who engraved the plate were different persons, the divergence was even more marked. Engravings can be prized for themselves: for their own formal beauty and their own technical accomplishment; and this is a legitimate pleasure. But the artist's original vision is seen, as it were, at one remove, through the net of another man's technique.

Etching, no doubt, at least in its great days, was more direct, and it is the triumph and the fascination of this process that it gives us a line even more free than is possible in a drawing, since the etching needle slips over the surface of the polished copper more easily than pen or pencil glides over paper. But what the artist does with the etching needle is still only the beginning. The plate must then, either by himself or another, be immersed in its bath of acid and suffer all the hazards of over- or under-biting. The printer must then intervene, and he can produce results so widely different that they would hardly be supposed to have stemmed from the same inspiration or be the work of the same hand. Nonetheless, etching remained, for a long time, the truest method of multiplying a work of art.

Then, at the very end of the eighteenth century, came Senefelder, and a whole world of new possibilities was opened up. Like many of the great inventions or discoveries, his was simply a new application of a natural principle. Oil and water do not mix! And it was a pleasant irony of the Time Spirit to make his notion spring from so tiresome and mundane matter as a laundry list. Senefelder was an aspiring dramatist and he wanted to print his plays himself. Like our own Blake he had experimented with methods of relief etching and it so happened that he had beside him a slab of the local Solenhofen stone:

> "I had just ground a stone plate smooth in order to treat it with etching fluid and to pursue on it my practice in reverse writing, when my mother asked me to write a laundry list for her. The laundress was waiting but we could find no paper. My own supply had been used up by pulling proofs. Even the writing-ink was dried up. Without bothering to send for writing materials, I wrote the list hastily on the clean stone with my prepared stone ink of wax, soap and lamp-black..."

What a happy combination of circumstances! But even then Senefelder did not tumble to the importance of what he was doing. He was still thinking in terms of etching away part of the surface of the stone, and printing, as Blake did, from the relief thus obtained. It was only later that he realised that this was unnecessary. All that was needed was to draw on a smooth (but not *too* smooth) stone with a greasy chalk, to wet the rest of the surface, to roll greasy ink over the whole (the wet portions of the surface repelling it) and then with the aid of a press to transfer the design thus created to paper.

It is not the purpose of a Foreword to enlarge on the technique of lithography, nor to dot the i's and cross the t's of an author who, by patient research, has cleared up so many of the problems of the early history of lithography. It is sufficient to hail the innovator who made so many later developments possible. For how many of the pictorial riches of the nineteenth century do we not owe to him?

Without the instrument which Senefelder put into his hand, the great Daumier might have been remembered only by a few small paintings. He could never have exercised his great political influence, never have shaken to its foundation the Throne of France. Without Senefelder our knowledge of French social life in the 'forties and 'fifties would have been immeasurably poorer by the absence of the lithographs of Gavarni. We should know far less of the Romantics of the 'thirties if Achille Deveria had never set down for us on the stone the form and features of young Dumas and his friends.

The nymph-haunted Arcadia of Fantin Latour would have been for ever closed to us; nor should we have been made free of the *coulisses* of the theatres of Paris in the company of Toulouse-Lautrec. The grey mists creeping over the Thames at Chelsea would never have found their most exquisite expression in the lithographic work of Whistler. None of these things should we have had if Senefelder had not been bothered, at an awkward moment, with a laundry list.

For all these artists found in lithography something which no other medium could give them. They found an immediacy, a possibility of direct approach which enabled them to catch the butterfly of their inspiration in flight. Lithography, especially in its latest developments, is so useful a technique that it can be used for all kinds of commercial reproductive purposes. The gay colours of hoardings and book-jackets—these too are Senefelder's work, and are not to be despised. But his great gift was to the graphic artist in making possible an uninhibited personal expression which could be multiplied forthwith without translation into terms of something else, without modification, deformation, or travesty. That is why his invention is still of interest to us, and why it is important for our understanding to have the early history of lithography accurately traced and set down for us: a task which Mr Man has so successfully accomplished in the present study.

JAMES LAVER

FOREWORD BY FELIX H. MAN

It has often happened in the past that a scientific discovery, though it may have been important, did not have the same influence as its practical application, which often only followed many years later.

How to produce a certain form of electricity on a minor scale had already been known to the Greeks without leading to any practical end for nearly two thousand years, until Faraday, in 1831, made his discovery of induction, to be followed by the inventions of Reis, Maxwell, Siemens, Hertz, from Edison to Marconi—inventions which now dominate our daily life.

The invention of lithography, though naturally only a minor one, took a different course.

When Aloys Senefelder, a Bavarian, produced his invention in 1798, which was by no means accidental but the result of many years of research and experiments, he was after a process suitable for multiplying plays, music and maps, and the first specimens of lithography are of this kind. But soon he himself and some artists realised the possibilities of this new method, and started to experiment with it here and on the Continent. Thanks to the great interest which Philipp André, brother of Senefelder's partner in Germany, showed towards this new 'Graphic Art', artists' lithography progressed first of all in England. This Philipp André had taken out a patent in England for the invention in August 1801, and soon afterwards sent stones to practically all living artists of reputation with the request for their contribution to a publication he finally issued as 'Specimens of Polyautography', as lithography was then called, on April 30, 1803.

Though the actual drawings for this publication had already been made partly in 1802 (one of them, Benjamin West's *Angel*, even in 1801), it is on this date of April 1803, one hundred and fifty years ago, when a number of original lithographs were published in a paper-covered folio as the first of a series to follow, that our chronology starts, as all previous attempts of artists, here and abroad must be regarded as purely experimental.

By restricting the history of lithography to the work of the *peintre-graveur* (there is no suitable word for this established French term) one arrives at practically a miniature history of art of the last one hundred and fifty years—as, with a few exceptions (at least, in France), nearly all great painters, sculptors and architects have practised this art.

When compiling such a history in pictures the number of available prints to choose from is naturally limited at the outset of this new graphic technique, and in order to show the development, some 'incunabula' of lesser artistic merit had to be included, as it took some time until all technical possibilities had been explored and perfected. However, Senefelder, the inventor, worked so thoroughly that he practically exhausted these himself within the first twenty years, and what we are doing today had all been foreseen by him and described in his own book in 1818, only perhaps with the difference that some of the material we are using now is somewhat refined. Though this present book is no technical treatise, I shall have to deal later with some of Senefelder's achievements, as they have been disputed again and again by people who have been misinformed.

A number of painters who did lithographs have been omitted, though at one time or another their work was greatly admired and the execution of their lithos was very good from the technical point of view. But, as in all the arts, technique should be only a medium to the end. With the real artist its mastering is self-understood and never a problem, because as a rule artistic conception matches technical ability. Rembrandt is not 'The Great Etcher' because he mastered his technique to the very end, but because, as a great painter and draughtsman, he moulded the technique of etching to attain this end.

In lithography the mixing of various technical possibilities such as chalk, pen, brush, scraper, and so on, for the purpose of obtaining an interesting texture, does not in itself raise the artistic value of a lithograph, nor is a print inferior because it is executed in one medium only. In the hands of a master no lithograph will ever be a mere multiplication of a drawing, as lithography, like all graphic arts, will always have its own characteristics.

Coming to the living painters and sculptors of today the choice had to be still more restricted, as their work had to stand up to that of a Géricault, a Delacroix or a Manet.

In recent years lithography, and especially colour lithography, has become very popular with the younger generation, and the public begins to realise that in acquiring a lithograph as wall decoration, they buy an original work of art. One of our modern artists, Kandinsky, had already written in 1926:[1] "By using more and more colour in lithography this technique comes closest to the hand-painted picture, at least it produces a certain substitute for the painting, which marks clearly the democratic nature of lithography". Perhaps in fifty years time, when the book *Two Hundred Years of Artists' Lithographs* will have been written, some prints of our young painters of today will be included.

★

The author wishes to thank all those who have kindly lent original prints for reproduction in this book or have given information to compile Section C.

A number of prints (all marked as such in Section C) have been lent by the British Museum Print Collection in London, by the Victoria & Albert Museum Print Collection in London, by Mr Rex Nan Kivell, Director of the Redfern Gallery in London, by the Galerie Louise Leiris and Monsieur H. Kahnweiler in Paris, and by Monsieur Tériade, Editor of *Verve* in Paris.

Permission to reproduce lithographs has been given by many of the living artists, by the *Guilde Internationale de la Gravure* in Geneva, by the Galerie Maeght in Paris, and by the Oslo Komunes Kunstsamlinger.

Special thanks are due to Mr James Laver, Keeper of Prints and Drawings at the Victoria & Albert Museum, as well as to Mr E. Seligmann, the book and print dealer in London, through whose foresight I was able to acquire for my collection a great number of rare lithographs, now reproduced in this book.

LONDON, *July* 1953.

[1] W. Kandinsky, *Punkt und Linie zu Fläche*, Munich 1926 (Author's translation).

SECTION A

7A. WILLIAM BLAKE, "JOB IN PROSPERITY", POLYAUTOGRAPH, *c.* 1807.

150 YEARS OF ARTISTS' LITHOGRAPHS

Though prints from stone had already been taken by Senefelder in 1796, and possibly still earlier by other people, the process we call lithography[1] today, and what is, in fact, chemical printing, was invented by Aloys Senefelder, a Bavarian, in 1798.

Senefelder himself wrote a long book on his invention,[2] the English version of which was published in 1819 by Ackermann in London, *A Complete Course of Lithography*, to which is prefixed a *History of Lithography from Its Origins to the Present Day*, from which the following quotations are taken:

"Lithography is a branch of a new method of printing, differing in its fundamental principles from all other methods now in use, and known by the name of Chemical Printing. All the other methods of printing hitherto known might be divided into two branches: the one multiplying the original by elevated forms, the other by engraved forms. To the first branch belongs the common letterpress printing, where the letters and signs are moulded in a composition of metal, or in wood, in such a manner that those lines and points which are to receive the colour, and be printed, are

[1] A definition of technical terms is found in Section C of this book.
[2] Senefelder, Aloys, *Vollständiges Lehrbuch der Steindruckerey*, Munich 1818.

elevated, while the rest of the plate, which is to remain blank on the paper, lies deeper. The wooden blocks for calico printing are of the same description.

Under the second branch may be included all the different methods of engraving on copper or tin, as well as calico printing from copperplates or cylinders. . . .

. . . It is evident that in both these methods of printing the charging of the types or plates with colour, by which the impression is obtained, depends entirely on mechanical principles, viz. that in the letterpress printing the colour adheres only to those places that come into contact with it, and in the copperplate printing to those from which it is not wiped off.

The chemical process of printing is totally different from both. Here it does not matter whether the lines be engraved or elevated, but the lines and points to be printed ought to be covered with a liquid, to which the ink, consisting of a homogeneous substance, must adhere, according to its chemical affinity and the laws of attraction, while at the same time all those places that are to remain blank must possess the quality of repelling the colour. These two conditions of a purely chemical nature are perfectly attained by the chemical process of printing; for common experience shows that all greasy substances, such as oil, butter, etc., or such as are easily soluble in oil, as wax, bitumen, etc., do not unite with any watery liquid without the intervention of a connecting medium, but that, on the contrary, they are inimical to water and seem to repel it. The principal dissolving and uniting liquid for the above-mentioned substances is alkali, which, by proper management, forms a sort of soap, soluble in water.

Upon this experience rests the whole foundation of the new method of printing which, in order to distinguish it from the mechanical methods, is justly called the *chemical method*; because the reason why the ink, prepared of a sebaceous matter, adheres only to the lines drawn on the plate and is repelled from the rest of the wetted surface, depends entirely on the mutual chemical affinity and not on mechanical contact alone.

It might perhaps be objected that in the other methods of printing the colour adheres to the lines which are to be printed, from the very same cause, as it is a well-known law, that water and oil adhere to all bodies in a perfectly dry state. But the case is not the same with fluids and their mutual effect, and this constitutes the essential difference between the former and this new method of print-ing. A dry plate would everywhere imbibe the colour; but the surface of the plate being wetted sufficiently, it takes the colour only on those places that are in a state the reverse of wetness. The repelling, therefore, of the colour from those places that are to remain blank is the novelty in the whole process."

This authentic record, which describes not only his original invention but also all those which followed within the next twenty years, is a historical document which leaves no doubt that Senefelder thought of everything possible that his method might be used for in the future; and, in fact, he left next to nothing for further improvement.

"The chemical process of printing is not only applicable to stone but likewise to metals, etc., and Lithography, therefore, is only to be considered as a branch of the more general chemical process of printing. . . .

. . . There are, besides, several other methods that are altogether peculiar to Lithography, and cannot possibly be imitated by type or copperplate printing. Of these I shall notice here only—first, the chalk manner, by which every artist is enabled to multiply his original drawings, and secondly, the transfer manner, by which every piece of writing or drawing with greasy ink on paper can be transferred to the stone and impressions taken from it."

A further invention he speaks of in his book is the 'Stone-paper'. He describes it as a stone-like substance "which can be formed by means of various compositions of clay, chalk, linseed oil and metallic oxides that when paper, canvas or wood are coated with it plates may be obtained capable of supplying the place of stone as a printing material . . ."

From these few extracts it becomes clear that Senefelder's inventive genius acted in an exhaustive way: substitutes for stone—stone-paper, metal plates, transfer paper—ideas and materials which in later years have been attacked as 'substitutes' and marked as 'not true lithography' by so-called 'experts' who did not care to study the facts. There was even an action about transfer-lithographs brought in the High Court by Pennell against Sickert, who sponsored the opinion that a lithograph made in this way is not an original. Pennell won, and transfer paper is used today by most important artists engaged in lithography.

A TRANSFER

Ackermann Lithography

23B. SAMUEL PROUT, TRANSFER LITHOGRAPH, 1818.

Though Senefelder is the inventor of all these processes, he did not give his child the name 'Lithography'. He originally called it 'Polyautography', or 'Chemical Printing', and the name 'Lithography did not appear for the first time until 1803–4, when it appeared, not in Germany, but in France. In his book *The Best and Only Collection of Incunabula of Lithography*[1] (Munich 1856), F. M. Ferchl claims that the word was first used in 1805 for the announcement of a work *Lithographische Kunstprodukte*. This claim, however, is incorrect (as are a number of other facts in this book, as Ferchl's observations are mainly limited to Bavaria). Pierre Nolasque Bergeret, a pupil of David, was already drawing in 1804 for a printing press set up in Paris a vignette depicting a Mercury with the words 'Imprimerie lithographique' underneath. The French collector and authority on early French lithographs, Monsieur Haslasz, recently showed me a piece of music printed from stone, with the description "Charenton près de Paris, à l'imprimerie lithographique", which he accepts as having already been printed in 1803. Though no date is printed on this piece of music, Monsieur Haslasz told me it had been registered in 1803 with the Bibliothèque Nationale, according to law. At all events, the word 'Lithography' was not created by Senefelder; it most probably spread all over Europe from France, and Senefelder in the end had to accept it, though always with reluctance and with reservations, stating clearly in his book: "Lithography is only to be considered as a branch of the more general process of chemical printing". When, in 1818, Quaglio drew Senefelder's portrait on stone (which is reproduced in this book facing the title page), he

[1] F. M. Ferchl, *Übersicht der besten und einzigen Incunabel Sammlung der Lithographie.* Munich 1856.

XV

had to write underneath: "Erfinder der Lithographie und der Chemischen Druckerey". Senefelder took this attitude in the proper assumption that, seen from the technical point of view, it was not the "stone" that mattered but the chemical process, compared with other methods of printing which were purely mechanical.[1]

The original idea behind Senefelder's invention was to find a cheap method of multiplication for industrial purposes. Art was not his *métier*, and he did not realise at the start the important part Lithography was to play within the 'Graphic Arts'.

The first attempt in this direction was made in 1800 by the Bavarian Count Törring-Seefeld, who drew views of the Lake of Wörth on stone, followed next year by experiments on similar lines by Professor Mitterer, together with his pupil Angelo Quaglio. All these attempts failed, however, as they did not know how to prepare the stone properly, nor did they know the secret of the correct printing ink.

A dilettante, E. J. Aurnhammer, who was a professor at the Gymnasium of Regensburg, drew twelve landscapes in 1802, and the stones were sent to Munich, where Senefelder took charge of the printing. However, only six survived and are rather meagre specimens. The same applies to two large landscapes by Mathias Koch, which he drew in 1802–3 at Offenbach-on-Main. They were executed on marble, and are rather coarse. Jakob Dorner drew a landscape in 1803, but this was not printed until 1806, and the painter Bauer made a portrait of the Prince-Primas Carl Dalberg in chalk. It was not until 1804, when Professor Hermann Mitterer opened the Kurfürstliche Druckerey at Munich, that a number of artists took greater interest in the new process in South Germany. This interest led to the publication in 1805, as mentioned before, of *Lithographische Kunstprodukte*, the artists being Andreas Seidl, Simon Klotz, Max Wagenbauer, and Simon Warnberger. This can be regarded as the first publication of artists' lithographs in South Germany.

In the meantime Senefelder, trying to commercialise his invention, accepted an offer made to him by the music publisher Joachim Anton André to come to Offenbach-on-Main to establish a press there and train suitable people in writing and printing. This connection led to a form of partnership, and on André's advice patents were taken out in various countries. In 1800 Senefelder went to London accompanied by André's brother Philipp; he stayed there for seven months, but was kept in the background by Philipp André, who was afraid that some of the secrets might leak out. About this London visit Senefelder writes:

> "The time passed in London, however, was not entirely lost for me and my art, for I employed my time in the study of chemistry . . . to improve my ink and other materials; I also made some progress in the aqua-tinta manner, in which Mr Gessner, son of the poet, an artist of talent, drew some pleasing landscapes. I am convinced that the public would have a greater number of masterly productions of the new art before them if it had been my fortune to have fallen in with an enterprising print-seller who employed proper artists. . . ."

Finally, in 1801, a patent was taken out and Senefelder departed, leaving Philipp André to establish a business. This Philipp André seems to have been the most efficient member of the family; he realised the latent possibilities of this new process and made it his main task to get artists of reputation interested in this new graphic art. He sent stones to many artists, together with the necessary instructions, and on April 30 1803 he was able to publish his first number of

> " Specimens of Polyautography,
> Consisting of Impressions taken from Original
> Drawings made purposely for this work.
> London: Published the 30th of April, 1803
> by P. André, Patentee, No. 5 Buckingham Street,
> Fitzroy Square, and J. Heath, 15 Russell Place, Fitzroy Square".

These prints are doubtless the first artists' lithographs ever to be published. However, neither the British Museum in London nor the Victoria & Albert Museum possesses a complete issue in the original

---

[1] A survey of what we now call 'Lithography' must, therefore, include everything printed in the chemical way, irrespective of the fact that scientists make a distinction between the various processes such as: Autography, Zincography, Algraphy, Transfer-Lithography, etc. There is no point in making these distinctions when assessing the artistic value of a print, just as it does not matter with an etching whether an iron, copper, zinc or nickel plate was used. The wrongly adopted name 'Lithography' now has to cover all methods of chemical printing or, better, 'Original Lithography' for the artists' work.

cover as published. In the print room of the Victoria & Albert Museum there is a folio to which someone has affixed the foregoing title. This folio contains twelve prints which, without doubt, were all published by André in 1803, but most probably in two parts of six each, following each other within two or three months. Some of these prints are dated 1802 by the artists; one, by Benjamin West, as early as 1801. This was the first artist's lithograph of merit ever to be made successfully. The prints are by Richard Cooper, 1802; R. K. Porter, 1803; Th. Barker of Bath; C. Gessner; Will. Dellamotte, 1802; H. Fuseli (Plate 3); Hearne; J. Barry; R. Courbauld, 1802; Warwick; Benjamin West (Plate 1), 1801; Th. Stothard (Plate 2).

There is a record of this publication in *Englische Miscellen*, published in Germany by Cotta at Tübingen, October 1803, Vol. XIII, Number 1, which reads in translation:[1]

"A novelty to be regarded with extraordinary interest are the first two numbers of 'Specimens of Polyautography', an invention of Aloys Senefelder, a German by birth, who holds a patent through Mr André. This German invention is of enormous importance for the arts."

The article then continues with a description of the technique and says: "The print is made from a completely flat surface". In a following paragraph it is announced that the price for one issue is half a guinea, and that it is intended to publish six issues containing six prints each. Well over thirty artists are named who were going to take part in the work, including Flaxman, Hoppner and Stubbs, who, however, never lithographed. André must, in fact, have asked practically everybody to explore this new art, and in the end have received more polyautographies than he could use. There are a number of prints known to have been designed in 1802, executed also with the pen, and in approximately the same size as those published—for instance, two by P. Bailey (Plate 4) and the "Tree" by Raphael Lamar West, the son of Benjamin West, reproduced here.

These twelve prints, published in 1803, were reissued in 1806 by G. J. Vollweiler, who had then taken over from André, and Ferchl must have seen one of these reprints, which led to his doubt that they were executed in 1802, since the watermark shows 1805.

In 1804 H. B. Chalon made a chalk drawing of some horses on stone (Plate 5) which can be regarded as the first successful drawing in chalk done by an artist, as previously only pen and ink had been used. Cooper then also used this medium (Plate 6), as did Fuseli in his second polyautography (Plate 7), which he made about 1806. Blake did his one and only polyautography, "Job in Prosperity", in about 1807 (reproduced on page xiii). Neither Constable nor Turner took any interest in this new art, but there are specimens by Cornelius Varley, J. Varley, Hills and other contemporary water colourists. Philipp André had left England in 1805; Vollweiler, his successor, published six issues in oblong folio, containing altogether thirty-six different prints, including some of the early ones. A complete copy of this publication is kept in the National Gallery of Berlin. In 1874 the print room of the British Museum acquired the Fisher Collection of British Incunabula of Polyautography, two large volumes containing about four hundred different prints,

[1] *Westdeutsche Bibliothek*, Marburg, Diesch Tv 4114 (Author's translation).

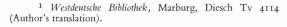

2A. R. L. WEST, "TREE", POLYAUTOGRAPH, 1802.

many by amateurs, for £7. 10s. 0d., which was a bargain. When Vollweiler gave up, a printer named Redmann took over and made it his business to encourage amateurs by supplying all the necessary material, including the stones on loan. Lithography, which had made such a splendid start in England ceased to exist as an art, with the exception of one publication worth mentioning: Thomas Barker of Bath, *Rustic Figures*, a publication in book form, brought out in 1813 by the artist himself by subscription.

This first publication of twelve polyautographies by André in 1803 had a certain influence on the development of artists' lithography in Germany.

7B.   TH. BARKER, "RUSTIC FIGURE", 1813.

Wilhelm Reuter, a painter living in Berlin, had been experimenting with lithography since 1801, and had done some small heads on stone which, however, were not very successful, as he did not have the necessary materials. Paul Hoffmann has written a vivid account of Reuter's merit in the cause of lithography, and this book, published in 1924,[1] is of special interest because it describes in detail Reuter's journey to Offenbach. There, when on his way to Paris in 1803, he first saw some English polyautographies. In Paris he met not only another of the André brothers but also the French artist Bergeret, about whom a detailed report will be given later on. Reuter was so impressed by these first English polyautographies that, on his return to Berlin, he decided to organise a similar publication. He invited the leading artists of Berlin to contribute, and managed to publish in September 1804 the *Polyautographische Zeichnungen vorzüglicher Berliner Künstler*, to which Reuter himself contributed two lithographs and signed as publisher. Other contributors were Professor Niedlich, Genelli and Schadow. All the drawings, done by pen, were still on marble as Solnhofener stone, the proper material, was not yet available in Berlin. As a whole, the result was feeble, only Schadow's drawing (Plate 9) commanding some respect. But Schadow, the sculptor and main representative in Germany of the classical period, was not only an artist of some stature but also a man experienced in other graphic arts. Between 1804 and 1837 he did nearly fifty lithographs (Plate 10), of which eleven were done on zinc. Mackowsky, who catalogued Schadow's graphic work anew in 1936, says that for these zinc lithographs Schadow used the following method: "A drawing is made with chemical ink on a paper with a grained surface, which is then damped and transferred on to a clean polished zinc plate by using a press. The zinc is then treated with phosphoric acid and a solution of gum, and then prints are taken from it in the same way as from stone." Schadow had already done this in 1827!

These polyautographic publications were continued by Reuter (Plate 8) for another three years and then lapsed.

Progress had, however, been made in developing the technical side of lithography in Germany, and Nepomuk Strixner opened a new field for lithography as a reproductive medium by copying Dürer's drawings for the Prayer Book of Emperor Maximilian, which were printed by Senefelder in 1808.

Other books and drawings followed until the reproductions of famous paintings from the galleries of Munich and other German towns became a vogue. Strixner, Piloty and Snyder were the main executors of this work. Senefelder's shop in Munich had become famous and was visited by princes,

[1] Paul Hoffmann, *Wilhelm Reuter, ein Beitrag zur Geschichte der Lithographie*, Berlin 1924.

XVIII

10A.   J. N. STRIXNER, PAGE 22 AND FRONTISPIECE FROM EMPEROR MAXIMILIAN'S PRAYER BOOK, DEL. 1807.

generals and the cream of society, and in 1809 he was appointed Inspector of the Royal Lithography Establishment in Munich. Lithography had become an industry in Germany.

Only a few artists took an interest in the process during the next few years. Karl Friedrich Schinkel, the architect of the classical period in Prussia, did a few prints, a very remarkable one in a large size in 1810, drawn with a pen (Plate 11); Angelo Quaglio, in 1812, a landscape with a Greek temple; his brother Domenico some Roman landscapes; Simon Klotz and Lorenz Quaglio some portraits; Peter Hess, Albrecht Adam, Dorner, Hosemann, the Swiss Töpfer, Karl Blechen the romanticist, Moritz von Schwind, Franz Krüger the Berlin court painter—these are the names to remember until the arrival of Adolf Menzel, a born lithographer (Plate 47). Though he made a start as a professional lithographer by assisting his father, his great natural gifts, his energy and his diligence made him the outstanding artist of his time in Germany. Though he did some remarkable work on stone throughout his long life, he also introduced professional wood-engraving on a large scale for illustrative purposes (*History of Frederick the Great*), which contributed largely to the extinction of lithography in that country.

In the meantime lithography as an art had been discovered in France, where the greatest living painters of their time produced drawings on stone, works of art unsurpassed in any other country.

The early publications of polyautography are not found in France as they are in England and Germany. After Frederic André's first start in February 1802 had become a failure—he was another member of the André family—several other attempts were made which shared the same fate; and it was not until 1809, when Vivan Denon, Dirécteur des Musées (Plate 14), went to Munich (where he drew "The Holy Family" on stone at Senefelder's shop) that lithography was officially encouraged in France. Before him Baron Lejeune, an artist and general in Napoleon's army, had been to Munich in 1806, where he drew his famous plate "The Cossack", one of the earliest French lithographs.

In his book *La Lithographie*, published in Paris in 1895, H. Bouchot, Librarian of the *Cabinet des*

Estampes, gives a chronological account of the French incunabula of lithography, as follows:
1. "Le Mercure," dessiné par Bergeret (1804).
2. Les portraits et les deux vues d'Angleterre, dessinés par le Duc de Montpensier en 1805 et 1806.
3. "Le Cosaque", dessiné par le Baron Lejeune en 1806 à Munich.
4. "Staininger", dessiné par le colonel Lomet en 1807.
5. "La Sainte Famille", dessiné par Denon en 1809.
6. Le portrait de Coupin de la Couperie, par Girodet-Trioson, en 1816.
7. "Le Paresseux, le Vigilant" et "l'Amour couché", exécutés par P. Guérin en aôut 1816.
8. "Un Lancier", dessiné par Horace Vernet en 1816.
9. Le Portrait de Mme. Perregaux, dessiné par le même en novembre, 1816.
10. Plusieurs portraits exécutés par Vivan Denon en 1816.

This list, made in 1895, is no longer correct, and certain modifications have been made, towards which two people contributed: Walter Gräff in *Die Anfänge der Lithographie in Frankreich*, Vienna, Gesellschaft für Vervielfältigende Kunst, 1904, and *Die Einführung der Lithographie in Frankreich*, Dissertation, Heidelberg, 1906, and Paul Hoffmann in his book about Wilhelm Reuter, Berlin 1924, previously mentioned. Hoffmann, who gives a detailed account of Reuter's journey to Paris in 1803 and what the artist encountered there, also prints a letter which Reuter wrote on December 13 1804 to the Trustees of the Berlin Academy for Fine Arts, addressed to H.E. von Hardenberg, Minister of State, which is preserved in the archives. This letter was written about a dispute between the Vice-Director, Frisch, and the Rector of the Academy, Schadow, about polyautography. It reads in translation:

"Towards the end of the last century (in fact 1803–*author*), at the request of a London art dealer, Monsieur André began to publish in monthly series the paintings and antiques of the Musée Napoléon in polyautography. . . . Monsieur Denon, Director-General of Museums, has agreed to choose the subjects. . . . During my stay in Paris (1803) a drawing after Rubens, a 'Deposition of Christ', had been finished . . . two others, after Poussin and Leonardo da Vinci, were nearly finished. The dealer has demanded that these should be drawn with the pen, and the piece I saw was very successful. . . . Monsieur André was somewhat embarrassed, as he had no news from England [because of the war]. It seems to me that he will not risk continuing this enterprise."

The plate reproduced here in this book reveals the name of the art dealer, Mr Bell, of Southampton Street, Strand, as well as the name of the artist who made the polyautographies, Pierre Nolasque Bergeret. Though Bergeret was the first artist to concern himself with lithography in France, the "Mercury" of 1804 is not French incunabula No. 1.

But all these early attempts were not followed up, and lithography became an entertaining pastime for Parisian society women and amateurs.

Not until Godefroy Engelmann set up a press at Mulhouse (1815), Count Lasteyrie in Paris (1815), and Engelmann also in Paris (1816), was lithography claimed by the fine arts.

While Lasteyrie at the beginning did only ordinary reproductive work of documents, etc., Engelmann approached artists like Vernet, Girodet, Regnault and Mongin and presented the fruits of their efforts to the Institut. The Institut appointed Pierre-Narcisse Guérin, a pupil of Regnault, as member of a commission to examine these lithographs submitted by Engelmann. In order to be able to pass judgment, Guérin himself executed a few lithographs, one of which is reproduced on Plate 13. Soon new printing establishments opened (Delpech, Motte, Gihaut and Lemercier) and new artists joined in: N. H. Jacob, both the Vernets, and Baron Gros (Plate 16), but most of these first lithographs were still rather feeble and partly of a silvery grey without colour.

One great painter, at that time living in Rome, had, unknown to his contemporaries, lithographed some portraits, four of them on to one large stone in 1815: John Dominique Ingres. These Ingres drawings, in all their delicacy, are masterpieces of the classical art of drawing. They are portraits on stone never repeated until Degas' experiments in lithography. They have not the weakness of all the other incunabula of lithography, as Ingres did not falter when faced with the new material for the first time. He remained Ingres, who drew as he painted and lithographed as he drew. With a precise stroke of his chalk he depicted his sitters. With an absolute certainty, and with a few sensitive lines, he brought out their character (Plate 12).

An Original slight Specimen Sketch of the manner of producing print Impressions from Drawings made on Stone Designed by Mr. Bergeret at PARIS.

Who is Employed to delineate the principal Pictures in the Gallery of the Louvre for periodical publication in Monthly Numbers by Mr. Bell at the Gallery of Arts, Southampton Street, Strand.

Printed at the Polyautographic Office No 5, Buckingham Street, Fitzroy Square, by P. André, the Patentee.

11B.   P. N. BERGERET, ADVERTISEMENT IN PEN LITHOGRAPHY, POLYAUTOGRAPH, *c.* 1803.

Though drawn in Rome in 1815, they were actually not printed until 1820, the noble family depicted having taken the stone to England, where Hullmandel took the impressions and added the titles. Only eight impressions are known so far of the four portraits printed on one sheet; even when in a cut-up condition these portraits must be described as rare. They are not listed by Bouchot in his catalogue of French incunabula of lithography, though in fact they are the most precious examples of early lithography in existence.

These four lithographs are so extraordinary that experts have been puzzled to know how it was possible for Ingres to have drawn them on the stone without previous experience of lithography, and some people—mainly in France—denounce them as not having been made by Ingres at all. They have developed a theory on this question, the main points being as follows:

(1) Ingres did the ordinary drawings on paper only, but not on the stone. Some years later the noble family had these drawings lithographed in England.
(2) These lithographs are not mentioned by Vicomte Henri Delaborde in his book and catalogue, *Ingres, sa vie, ses traveaux, sa doctrine*, Paris 1870.
(3) A chemical drawing on stone done in 1815 would not stay perfect all these years (5–10 years) without deteriorating through atmospheric influences.
(4) It was Richard Lane, the engraver and lithographer, who drew the Ingres portraits on stone, as he copied Gainsborough's sketch-book in lithographic technique most excellently.

I have examined these points most carefully and come to the following conclusions: Ingres could have made these lithos himself in 1815 only if he had the necessary facilities in Rome at that time. There is documentary evidence that a certain Giovanni Dall'Armi received a licence on January 4 1808

XXI

to open a printing and publishing establishment for lithography in Rome.[1] Therefore Ingres had the necessary facilities. How, then, is it possible that he achieved this perfection in his first lithographs? The technique is comparatively easy for a draughtsman of the calibre of Ingres and, as long as he made a straightforward drawing, should not have contained any pitfalls. (It must also be remembered that the technique and the quality of the materials, the stones, etc., had already been highly developed in neighbouring Germany, whence supplies came to Rome.) Ingres approached the stone in the same way as paper. He was not frightened of it, and it is quite possible that he made a few tests first at the printer's mentioned before. Though he had already achieved some fame by 1815, he was only thirty-five years old—and every scrap of paper an artist used was not collected at that time!

The idea of having these lithographs done probably originated with the North family, as at that time the nobility in England took a great interest in lithography as amateurs (the Duchess of Montrose, Lord Cawdor, Lady Georgiana North, Lady Long). As mentioned earlier, a straightforward chalk drawing on stone presented no problem, and certainly not to a man who six months later, in 1816, managed to do an etching, also without previous experience: the portrait of Monsignore Gabriel Cortois de Presigny, a masterpiece of that period not disputed by experts. No examples of this far more difficult technical process done by Ingres exist before or after this one portrait! This clearly shows that technical difficulties did not exist for an artist like Ingres. If we look at Géricault's work in lithography we also note that those stones he executed at the beginning, in 1818, are superior to those he did later when he became lithograph-conscious; they are bold and free in his own style of drawing. The same is true of Ingres: the two lithographs he did in later years, "Les Quatre Magistrats de Besançon" for the *Work of Baron Taylor* and his "Odalisque" in 1825, do not attain the quality of his portraits.

Why, then, are these English portraits not mentioned by Vicomte Delaborde in his catalogue of Ingres' work? Because this catalogue is not exhaustive. If Ingres had done the drawings on paper and not on stone, they would have been catalogued in the same book. But they are not.

It is nonsense to assume that a stone would not last five to ten years without suffering considerably. Delacroix did the lithographs of his medals in 1825 (Plate 34), but they were not published until 1864, after his death.

The last question to be cleared up is, that if somebody else had done the drawings on stone later in England after Ingres' originals, who was it? Certainly not Richard Lane. Lane was an excellent engraver and copyist. His imitations of "Studies of Figures by Gainsborough" were published in January 1825 with Lane's name as large as Gainsborough's. All Lane's lithographic work has his name affixed to it, even minute specimens. Lane was born in 1800. He became an apprentice to Charles Heath in 1816 to learn engraving. He remained an engraver until 1824, when he took up lithography. The Ingres lithographs, however, were printed in 1820; they were printed by Hullmandel on Whatman paper. I have examined three complete sheets with the four portraits; they were all on the same paper, one of them having the watermark "Whatman 1820".

[1] Guiseppe Fumagalli, in *Rivista della Stampa*, Rome 1937. (Another book, by Leandro Ozzola, *La Lithografia Italiana*, Rome 1923, even contains a description of this Dall'Armi having printed for Ingres, an assumption probably correct but not proved.)

There is, however, another peculiarity I noticed on these sheets. Until the middle of 1821 Hullmandel, the printer, was in the habit of signing the prints coming from his establishment with "C. Hullmandel's Lithography". After that date he changed to "Lithography by C. Hullmandel" or "Printed by C. Hullmandel". The Ingres prints bear the imprint "C. Hullmandel's Lithography". But there is still another peculiarity: the "d" in the word "Hullmandel" has the little stroke on the top facing towards the right *d* and not, as is usual, facing left. This curious form of the letter "d" does not exist at any later date, but only on prints of the year 1820 and the beginning of 1821.

(D O U G L A S) L O R D

Nat. 13. May O.S. 1744.

C. Hullmandel's Lithography.

From all these facts it is evident and conclusive that the Ingres lithographs were printed by Hullmandel in 1820 (as the watermark shows) or during the first half of 1821 at the latest (as the signature and the "d" show). How, then, could Richard Lane have done the stones? At that time he was only twenty years old, had done no lithographs before, and was still an engraver. And if Lane did not do them, who else could have copied Ingres with such mastery—except Ingres himself? There was no lithographer at that time in England who had this ability.

★

In France after 1817, when a good number of printing establishments had been set up, lithography progressed rapidly in popularity and was officially acknowledged as an art practised by a number of painters. Carle Vernet and his son Horace (Plate 15) did many designs, though they are for the greater part forgotten today.

An interesting document written by Louise Pujol, the wife of Horace Vernet, whom he had married in 1811, shows that lithography must have become very popular indeed with the public.[1] This document lists all the earnings of Horace Vernet from the day of his marriage until his death in 1863. Part of it reads:

1817	Mars 7.	Un dessin lithogr. pour M. de Lasteyrie.	Frcs. 120
1818	Fev. 18.	Une lithogr. pour M. Delpech.	Frcs. 600
	Juillet 29.	Une lithogr. pour Mme Delpech.	Frcs. 800

and the same year, in November:

Une lithogr. pour M. de Forbin   Frcs. 1,000

By 1822 his price for a lithograph had risen to Frcs. 1,500 each, and his income from lithography alone in 1822 was Frcs. 9,000, which was a large sum of money in those days.

★

The genius who stands near the threshold of modern painting, Theodore Géricault, a pupil of Guérin, influenced lithography decisively. As a reaction from David, who had dominated painting in France for nearly twenty-five years, the romantic movement, with Géricault at its head, rendered life in a new and thrilling way, in vivid and exciting colours. It was Géricault who, in the real sense, first achieved colour in black-and-white lithography. His first stones date from 1817, but already in 1818 he had designed some of his best work: "Deux chevaux se battant dans une écurie", "Artillerie à cheval changeant de

[1] Armand Dayot, *Les Vernets*, Paris 1898.

position" and "Mameluck défendant un trompette blessé" (Plate 17). In these lithographs colour is really transposed and expressed, the design is bold and powerful. Another stone, "Les Boxeurs", and some of the lithographs he did during his stay in England come into the same class (Plates 18 and 19).

While all this progress was being made in France nothing of importance had happened in England since the Gentlemen of Bath had taken over, after the first promising start in 1802–6.

Finally, in 1818, Charles Hullmandel published an album, *Twenty-four Views of Italy*, printed by Moser. Hullmandel had studied the technique of lithography right at the source at Senefelder's establishment, and after the publisher and print-seller (Ackermann) had printed and published Senefelder's book in 1819, and Hullmandel had set up his own press in London, the technical possibilities existed for similar progress as had been made in France. The leading artists, Constable and Turner, however, had no interest in this "democratic" process, and it was a French artist, Géricault, who delivered the first stones of high artistic merit to Hullmandel's new establishment.

He came to England together with his friend Nicolas Toussaint Charlet for the exhibition of his painting "Shipwreck of the Medusa". During his stay he designed twelve stones, "Various Subjects drawn from Life on Stone", printed by Hullmandel and published by Rodwell and Martin, February to May, 1821, generally known as the English set (Plates 18 and 19).

At the same time, while in London, Géricault also made some experiments with Senefelder's latest invention by making some drawings in pen and ink on stone-paper, a substitute for stone, one of which is reproduced here.

19A.   TH. GÉRICAULT, LITHOGRAPH PRINTED FROM STONE-PAPER, 1820.

While in London Géricault met, among others, James Ward, whom he admired very much, and whose work had a certain influence on his later painting. But Ward himself, a painter of great gifts belonging to the English romantic school, who is still underrated today, was doubtless inspired by Géricault's English set of lithographs, and soon afterwards he drew a series of fourteen very remarkable lithographs, "Celebrated Horses", which he published himself in 1823 and 1824 (Plate 24). Some of these lithographs are full of colour, the form and technical execution also being excellent. Had they been done in France by a French artist they would today be hailed as masterpieces of lithography.

At the same time another Englishman, Richard Parkes Bonington, a friend of Delacroix, did some very remarkable work on stone. Bonington spent the greater part of his short artistic career in France, where he contributed lithographs to Baron Taylor's mammoth publication, *Voyage Pittoresque en France* (Plate 28), some of which were printed in England by Hullmandel. Inspired by this work, Hullmandel issued similar folios: Prout's "Rhine", "Foreign Views", and a combined work of Harding, Westall, Hullmandel and Prout, *Britannia Delineata*.

Hullmandel also published a book in 1824, *The Art of Drawing on Stone*. In the introduction he gives an account of the difficulties lithography had to overcome in England:

"In France, Bavaria and in Russia the respective Governments have introduced and fostered lithography, and it is much to be regretted that in this country, where this pleasing duty is generally left to noblemen and private individuals of fortune, no patron of the arts has hitherto stepped forth to promote this beautiful discovery. . . . It is, indeed, rather curious to compare the behaviour of the two governments in this single instance. When lithography first appeared in Germany the French Government sent two agents to that country to examine the merits of the new discovery and to endeavour to introduce it into France. . . . On the other hand, when the infant art was introduced into England an almost prohibitive duty was laid on the very material, viz. the importation of stones. . . ."

Another passage reads:

"Luckily, however, for lithography, instead of being despised and abused by artists of talent (in France), as it is continually and most strangely done here, men of real merit have taken it in hand . . . and have produced such specimens as must astonish all those who see them. It is hoped that lithography will also some day meet in England with that support which it deserves . . . and that those persons who now call it a mean art will use a portion of the great and real talent which they possess towards producing specimens that may at least equal what is now done on the Continent! . . . Prints of every description find purchasers in France amongst those classes of society which in England view them with as much concern as they would hieroglyphics. The understanding, taste and knowledge of the Fine Arts has within the last thirty years wonderfully spread amongst the middling orders in France, and has also made great progress in England since a few years. . . ."

Thomas Bewick, famous through his woodcuts, tried his hand only once on stone, doing a sketch, "The Cadger's Trot", in 1823. Bewick himself writes in his memoirs about this, his only attempt to lithograph:

21st August 1823.

"Whilst I was at the office of Messrs. Ballantyne and Robertson, Lithographic printers (in Edinburgh), the latter pressed me to make a sketch on the stone for him. I was then preparing to leave Edinburgh, and the only time left me was so short that I was obliged to draw this sketch before breakfast the next morning, and the Proofs were taken from it on the same day. In doing this, though very slight, I could see what that manner of making prints was capable of. I left Edinburgh on the 23rd August 1823."

However he must have taken some pain over this lithograph, as the various states, which exist, now are showing (Plates 26 and 27).

David Octavius Hill, painter and past-master of photography, lithographed a number of landscapes from 1821 to 1823. They are, however, of less importance than his photographs (Plate 25).

There are still two miniature lithographs done by Edward Calvert in 1829 which should be mentioned. They are very similar in style to his well-known woodcuts which he did under the influence of his friend Blake. The third man in this trio of friends, Samuel Palmer, did no lithographs, though he practised etching widely and most brilliantly.

The lithographed work of J. F. Lewis ("Sketches of Spain"), John Nash ("Architecture"), G. Cattermole and T. S. Boys is not very convincing, and does not compare in any way with the lithographs produced in France during the same period. In his book on lithography Pennell says that the British painters avoided lithography out of sheer snobbishness. This may have been partly true, but it was to a greater extent due to the fact that the leading painters of the second half of the century were French, that no lithos of importance were produced in England until the American-born Whistler and the half-English Sickert took a hand in it.

In Russia lithography became known much later than in Central or West European countries, and it was not until 1815 that a press was set up in St Petersburg (Leningrad); this was first used only for the reproduction of documents. The Polish-born painter Alexander Orlowski, who had settled in St Petersburg, was the first to take an interest in the new art, and his first published lithographs appeared in 1816: a Turk from Turkestan and three horsemen from Kurdestan. Baron G. v. Schilling, from Livland, who had learned the art from Senefelder in Munich, followed his lead by establishing himself as a publisher of lithographs. By 1819 this same Orlowski had done some very large prints depicting Russian life in town and country, and soldiers in picturesque uniforms from the Caucasus and other more remote parts of this vast country. These prints were not only executed in a most brilliant technique, as Orlowski was a very accomplished draughtsman, but also showed great understanding of the art of expressing colour with the black chalk (Plates 22 and 23).

★

At about the same time as in Russia lithography had been introduced into the United States of America, and the portrait painter Bass Otis carried out experiments in 1818–19 in this new method. His small landscape drawings, which were published in the *Analitic Magazine* in Philadelphia in 1820, are generally accepted as the first American lithos, though Pennell reports in his book that a lithograph signed "Benj. Otis" was published in the same magazine in 1819. The Journal of the Franklin Institute published a detailed description of the technique of this new art, and offered a prize in 1827 for the best lithograph executed in the States. This was won by Rembrandt Peale for his large portrait of Washington. Other American artists who did lithographs in these days were Thomas Cole, Doughty and Professor Schussele, and, after the revolution of 1848, la Farge, W. H. Hunt and Winslow Homer. The work of all these painters had, however, no influence on the development of lithography as an art. This was left to those American-born artists who spent the greater part of their careers in Europe, such as Benjamin West, J. M. Whistler, Mary Casatt, Sargent and Pennell.

28A. BASS OTIS, EARLY AMERICAN LITHOGRAPH, 1820.

Towards the end of his life Pierre Paul Prud'hon, the "Correggio of the Empire", did three lithographs, of which only "Une Lecture" embodies the real Prud'hon, who, in his paintings, understood so well how to elicit a seductive and significant smile from a woman's face, as only Leonardo had done before (Plate 21).

From Géricault the line of succession leads directly to Delacroix, his friend and heir, but it went via Goya, the great Spanish painter and etcher, who, in his old age, in 1819, had started to lithograph. While in voluntary exile in Bordeaux he executed his set of four stones: "Los Toros de Burdeos" (The Bulls of Bordeaux), so called because they were executed in Bordeaux from memory as no bull-fights of this kind took place in that town. Goya himself called these masterpieces "Diversion d'España" (Plates 29 and 31). At the same time he drew some smaller pieces of great excellency (Plates 30 and 32).

Though Delacroix had earlier made some drawings on stone—some caricatures in 1820 and various stones with some antique medals in 1825 (Plate 34), a decisive change in conception and technique becomes visible in his seventeen lithographs, illustrating Goethe's *Faust*, which were published in 1828 by Motte (Plate 33). In these stones he masters lithography in a most powerful and dramatic way, his stroke of the chalk is much bolder, resulting in greater artistic unity. Doubtless he had seen the Goyas and profited from this experience. Some of his later work, the celebrated "Lion d'Atlas" and "Tigre Royal", are of greater virtuosity and perhaps more anatomically correct than *Faust*. One of his best plates of this period, however small, is "Jeune Tigre jouant avec sa mère" (Plate 35), published in *L'Artiste* in 1831, when this journal was founded by Ricault. He also did lithographs for *Macbeth*, *Hamlet* and *Goetz*, as well as a great number of single stones, totalling about one hundred pieces.

During the romantic period in France lithography occupied first place within the graphic arts and dominated etching. Perhaps this was caused by Géricault, as well as Delacroix, opposing in a certain sense colour to line.

Théodore Chassériau, pupil of Ingres and later a disciple of Delacroix, did only three lithographs, two of them of rare quality. Chassériau's art is a connecting link between his two masters. The beautiful slim bodies of his figures create a sensual atmosphere, passionate like the colour of Delacroix and cool like the classical design of Ingres (Plate 41).

As always in time of political depression, the glorification of the past offers a kind of retreat and consolation. The Napoleonic Legend, the *Grande Armée*, the battles and the life of the soldier therefore offered substance for numberless lithographs, eagerly snapped up by the public. Nicolas Toussaint Charlet (Plate 20), Hippolyte Bellangé, Auguste Raffet, and even Géricault, are the principal representatives of this genre.

Contemporary life was illustrated by Monnier, Lami and Victor Adam, while Louis Boilly lithographed *Les Grimaces*, a sequence of ninety-six stones, published by Delpech between 1822 and 1826.

Portrait lithography found its greatest exponent in Achille Deveria, whose "Alexandre Dumas père" (Plate 37) and "Victor Hugo" are convincing examples of his art.

Eugène Isabey issued *chez Morlot à Paris*, his famous *Cahiers de Marine*, coastal scenes, ports and cliffs, painted in black chalk (Plate 38), published simultaneously in London by MacLean and in New York by Bailly.

The important romantic landscape painter Paul Huet, a pupil of Gros and Guérin, had a more lyrical approach to his subject and used the chalk with greater tenderness and refinement than Isabey, thus achieving effects of a poetical nature (Plate 39).

Jules Dupré's few lithographs were published in the early numbers of *L'Artiste*. They are interpretations of his own paintings, but not copies. He was a friend of Théodore Rousseau, and was influenced by Constable, whose work he knew well from a visit to England. The Forest of Fontainebleau offered him many motives (Plate 40).

Diaz de la Pena, a painter who also worked in the Forest of Fontainebleau, and who is somewhat neglected today, did a number of lithographs of a certain sensual charm mixed with a fairy-like atmosphere (Plate 42). The influence of Prud'hon is clearly visible in his work but assimilated into his own style.

Some of Antoine Louis Barye's lithographs, who, although a sculptor, also painted occasionally in the Forest of Fontainebleau, were also published in *L'Artiste*. They are animals—tigers, bears and stags—

of a great strength of form, executed in a plain and clear way, of a certain magnitude peculiar to the sculptor (Plate 36).

Jean François Millet, the master of Barbizon, did only three lithographs, of which "Le Semeur", executed in 1851, is the most important.

★

The revolution of 1830 and the ease with which thousands of impressions can be taken from a stone are the two factors which created Daumier the 'lithographer'.

Charles Philipon, originally a lithographer of some mediocrity, founded *La Caricature* in 1830, to be followed by *Le Charivari* in 1832. Daumier's lithographic work, which numbers over four thousand pieces, was published in these two papers over a period of forty years. He joined *La Caricature* in 1831, and the most important and famous contributions of his early period came in the years 1833–5: "Guizot" (Plate 43), "Le Ventre Législative", "Enfoncé Lafayette", "La Rue Transnonain" and "La Tête Branlante" (Plate 44). The work of this early period is very different from his later work, not only because it is entirely political, but because in his design he shows far more the conception of a sculptor than that of a painter. In fact, he was in the habit of modelling his heads before drawing them. What makes Daumier's caricature so powerful is that he never becomes grotesque, but arrives at a certain monumental quality by enlarging the typical, always thinking in volumes. When *La Caricature* ceased to exist Daumier's work in *Le Charivari* became a kind of satire on the life of the *petit bourgeois*; his style changed, first to a more pronounced outline and then to lithographs of real painter-like quality. His creations of the series "Robert Macaire", "Les Baigneurs", "Les Gens de Justice" and "Actualités" must be seen in proof state in order to assess them, as *Charivari* was printed on ordinary newsprint, the reverse shining through.

Among his last lithographs are those in the *Album de la Siège*, published in 1871 (Plate 45).

Of Daumier's contemporaries, Grandville, Andrieux, Beaumont and Gavarni, only the last named has survived. Originally a regular contributor to *La Mode* and a creator of fashion design, he later became Daumier's colleague at *Le Charivari*, where his "Lorettes" were published. His series "Le Manteau d'Arlequin", published by the short-lived journal *L'Eclair* (Plate 46), belongs to his later work.

For nearly twenty-five years these caricaturists were the only creative lithographers in France, as lithography had become merely a medium for professionals whose aim was to translate painters' work into black-and-white for reproduction by this method. Even the magazine *L'Artiste*, founded for the purpose of publishing artists' original lithographs, had ceased to publish originals, the reproductive craftsmen having taken over.

The French publisher Cadart, who initiated a renaissance of etching in France, tried to do the same with lithography. In 1862 he asked Manet, Ribot, Fantin-Latour and Legros to do some lithographs for him. Manet, by far the most important artist of the four, did "Le Ballon". The soft chalk suited this great painter better than the etching needle, and though "Le Ballon" remained unpublished, he continued to use the stone, doing about a dozen more lithographs in the next seven years, including a large poster, "Le Rendez-vous des Chats", to advertise Champfleury's book on cats, and "L'Exécution de Maximilian", all good drawings with fine feeling for colour. His style changed, however, with "La Guerre Civile" and "La Barricade" (Plate 48), scenes from the civil war in 1871 which he had actually witnessed. Quite a new conception becomes visible, which is still more perceptible in "Course à Longchamp", a lithograph "in shorthand" (as Curt Glaser remarks[1]), an attempt to demonstrate fast action in a novel way, instigated probably by Goya's "Taureaux".

★

In the meantime transfer paper, already invented by Senefelder, had been greatly improved, and when, in 1874, Manet illustrated Mallarmé's translation of Edgar Allan Poe's *The Raven* with six lithographs drawn with the brush, he used this method (Plate 49). These lithographs show clearly the influence of Japanese art on Manet and his friends of the Café Guerbois. The World Fair of 1867, where a large selection of Japanese colour-prints was on view, had publicised this art from the East which, from

[1] Curt Glaser, *Die Graphik der Neuzeit*, Berlin 1923.

then onwards, was to influence practically all nineteenth-century painters and, above all, colour lithography in the 'nineties.

Manet's contemporaries, however, did not appreciate *The Raven*, printed in a limited edition on large paper. The publication remained unsold and other plans had to be abandoned. He also did a lithograph in colour, "Polichinelle", at the same time, a novelty of its kind. Daumier excepted, Manet was the first painter of standing since Delacroix to concern himself with the stone, and he must be regarded as the father of modern lithography and book illustration.

Corot, who never mastered the technical side of etching, found lithography, and especially transfer-paper, suited his purpose, using chalk and pen with the same mastery and economy as in his drawings of fairy-like landscapes, of which Meier-Graefe[1] writes: "There are no motionless motives in the work of this singer of solitude. Things which really keep still—he brings to life." And Corot himself said: "Il me faut un modèle qui remue".[2] Corot executed these little masterpieces in his old age in 1871–4. (Plate 50).

Edgar Degas, today cherished as 'the great graphic artist' of the last century, also experimented with lithography, doubtless inspired by Manet. From 1875 onwards he executed a number of stones of great beauty and outstanding graphic qualities. He invented his own process[3] whereby he made his design with a brush and ink on a blank copperplate, taking an impression of it on transfer-paper (monotype). The printer transferred this to the stone, on which Degas then worked with chalk, scraper, etc., continuing to build up the lithograph over a great number of states, a method he liked very much, as in this way he obtained different and new effects (Plate 60). His graphic work remained practically unknown to the general public until his death, as his plates and stones were not published. They are real gems.

These attempts by Manet, Corot and Degas to revive lithography bore no real fruits, however, until the last decade of the century, though Fantin-Latour and Redon occupied themselves a good deal with this art.

Odilon Redon published his first album, *Dans le Rêve*, in 1879. Though a friend of the Impressionists, he found "the ceiling of Impressionism is too low". His aim was *"La beauté humaine avec le prestige de la pensée"*. To some extent he belongs to the Symbolists, but at the same time he must be regarded as a forerunner of the Surrealists, and he wrote: *"Rien ne se fait en art par la volonté seule. Tout se fait par la soumission docile à la venue de l'inconscient"*[4] (Plates 52 and 53).

Fantin-Latour, pupil of Courbet, who did only two lithographs, did not adopt his master's realistic notion; on the contrary, most of his lithographs are "fantastic". He illustrated Berlioz and Wagner, showing surprisingly little taste in these plates. Some of his nudes and his flower-piece "Bouquet de Roses", however, will survive, as do his paintings on these subjects (Plate 51).

Paul Gauguin, whose graphic work mainly consists of exciting woodcuts in his own technique, partly in colour, published a series of lithographs in 1889, after he had passed Impressionism. They were exhibited the same year at the Café Volpini in Paris, together with works by Emile Bernard, Schuffenecker, Laval and Anquetin, described as "Le Groupe Impressioniste et Synthétiste". Fifty copies only of this series of ten lithographs by Gauguin, scenes from Martinique, Arles and Brittany (Plate 56) done on zinc, were printed in the original edition on yellow paper of strong colour. A reprint was made later on *simili Japon*. When Gauguin returned to Paris in 1894, between his two stays in Tahiti, he executed "Manuo Tupapau" (Plate 55) for Vollard's album. The proofs are signed and numbered in ink, one hundred altogether.

★

Colour which, in purified state, played a foremost part in the paintings of Manet and the open-air pictures of the Impressionists, also found its way into lithography. Since the publication of Manet's "Polichinelle" and Jules Chéret's first poster in polychrome for the Bal Valentino in 1869, the technique of colour printing of lithographs had been greatly improved. Under the supervision of experienced

[1] Jul. Meier-Graefe, *Entwicklungsgeschichte der Modernen Kunst*, Munich 1903.
[2] A. Robaut et Moreau Nelaton, *L'Œuvre de Corot*, Paris 1904.
[3] This process is described by Denis Rouart in *Degas à la recherche de sa technique*, Paris 1945.
[4] Odilon Redon, in his remarkable journal *A Soi Même*, Paris 1922.

printers like Cotelle, Clot and Stern, those magnificent results were finally obtained which in our present day are sought after at fantastic prices by museums and collectors.[1]

Colour lithography is a very specialised job. A separate stone is necessary for each colour, and the final result depends on the co-operation of painter and printer far more than in black-and-white work. Though it is naturally the artist's task to prepare the stones for all colours, it is the printer's skill in mixing and applying these colours which decides whether the painter's aims are finally achieved.

The renaissance of lithography came in the eighteen-nineties, originating in colour. Toulouse-Lautrec did his first poster in polychrome ("Moulin Rouge") in 1891, followed by "La Goulue et sa Sœur" (Plate 58) and "L'Anglais au Moulin Rouge" in 1892. The success of these first colour prints resulted in Lautrec doing over 350 lithographs within ten years: posters, programmes, illustrations, single prints in colour and black-and-white, scenes from Moulin Rouge, dancers, actors, cabaret stars, café concerts, racecourses, animals—the themes he liked best (Plate 57). In his series *Elles* (1896), a portfolio, he used colour lithography for the first time for such a publication, with a purely artistic aim.

During this period all painters, with the exception of Monet, lithographed, supported by publishers like Sagot, Kleinmann, Pellet and Vollard. In 1893 Marty founded *L'Estampe Originale* for the purpose of publishing lithographs, Vollard started his *Albums des Peintres-Graveurs*, *L'Escarmouche* was founded in 1893, *La Revue Blanche* in 1890, and *L'Estampe et l'Affiche* in 1897 by Mellerio.

Bonnard, Vuillard, Signac, Cross, Luce, Gauguin, Renoir, Pissarro, Cézanne, Denis, Roussel, Puvis de Chavanne, Guillaumin, Redon, Carrière (Plate 54), Sisley, Rodin, Maillol, Forain, Whistler, and others, all did lithographs for Vollard, the art dealer, who took a special interest in colour lithography. In some respects, however, he overshot the mark, when he persuaded Cézanne, Renoir and Sisley to work in colour. In fact, these artists only did the work on the black stone, giving Clot, the excellent master-printer, a tinted copy from which he did the colour stones. But this comes closer to facsimile reproduction than original lithography.

Sisley did only one original lithograph himself (Plate 64), and of Cézanne's prints only the self-portrait (Plate 61) is an original. The same applies to Rodin's lithographs, which, as Delteil confirms, are partly done by Clot after Rodin's drawings.

Renoir's graphic art plays only a minor part in his life's work. His etchings were mainly done as frontispieces for books, and the soft ground suited him best. He did some portraits in lithography of which "Wagner" (Plate 66) is more free and fluid in treatment, and his "Cézanne" is one of his best. The great stones like "Chapeau épinglé" (a repetition of several etchings), "L'enfant au biscuit" and "Enfants jouant à la Balle" are among those executed in collaboration with Clot. Seventy-five copies of "Odalisque", a small lithograph of great charm, were printed as frontispiece for a book never published (Plate 65). He also did some drawings on stone for an album, published by Vollard.

Of the Impressionists only Pisarro took greater interest in the graphic arts and his etched work is very extensive. He did his first ten lithographs about 1874, all on transfer paper, but then paused until 1896, when his art had overreached the ordinary conception of the Impressionism of his earlier days. He was then acquainted with Seurat and Signac, and had painted in their manner for a period. His life-long experience and a more constructive outlook are reflected in these later lithographs, and his series of "Baigneuses", done in fine tints and chalk, show him at his best (Plate 63).

The Néo-Impressionists, often wrongly described as Pointillists (Seurat, Signac, Cross, etc.), with the exception of Seurat, made an important contribution to colour lithography.

"Le néo-impressioniste ne pointille pas, mais divise."[2]

As medium of expression they used the optical combination of colour and tints, a luminous and pure colouring of integral harmony, as shown by the prism. Their method of absolute division of colour was most suitable for lithography and the colour prints of Signac and Cross, though they have not the sound architectural basis of Seurat's painting, are among the finest specimens of colour lithography.

In 1888 a number of artists—Bonnard, Vuillard, Denis, Ranson and Sérusier—met at the Academy Jullian. This later resulted in the formation of a group, baptised by the poet Cazalis as "Nabis". Maurice Denis, though a painter, was at the same time an experienced writer, and he became their spokesman. Other members were Roussel (interested in mythology), Vallotton (Swiss by birth), Ranson, Ibels,

[1] *See* Section "C": Lautrec, Signac, Bonnard, Vuillard.
[2] Paul Signac, *D'Eugène Delacroix au Néo-Impressionisme.*

Verkade and Maillol. Their meeting-place became *La Revue Blanche*, and most of these artists did lithographs for this magazine.

"The arranging of colour in a certain order", as Maurice Denis put it, to achieve organization in painting, was one of the principles of the "Nabis". Their contribution to painting was of less importance at that time than their contribution to colour lithography, which, as already mentioned, was about to become an important factor as a medium of expression for the artists of that period.

Though originally belonging to the "Nabis", Bonnard treated their dogma more freely. Strongly influenced by Japanese colour prints, he developed his own style in colour lithography, his first important work in that line being published by Vollard in 1895, "Quelque Aspects de la vie de Paris", a set of twelve lithos in colour depicting scenes in Paris, published one year before Toulouse-Lautrec's "Elles". He also contributed to *La Revue Blanche*, *L'Escarmouche* (Plate 67), and to Vollard's *Albums des Peintres-Graveurs*. In 1900, when his style had become more refined, he lithographed "Les Boulevards" for the *German Insel Mappe* (Plate 68). He also illustrated *Parallèlement* for Vollard in 1900 and *Daphnis et Chloé* in 1902 with lithographs. He continued to draw on the stone until his death in 1947 (Plate 69).

The lithographs of his friend and 'fellow-traveller', Vuillard, number sixty pieces. His set, "Paysages et Intérieures" was published in 1899 by Vollard (Plate 71). His lithographs are of a strong composition, often using the decorative element of the wallpaper pattern and showing a very refined colour sense. His black-and-white work is brilliantly executed (Plate 70).

Maurice Denis' lithographs, long neglected, are now making a come-back and are again widely appreciated (Plate 72).

One figure difficult to place because of his internationality—born American, domiciled in England, often working in France, where he exhibited at the Salon des Réfusés together with Manet, Jongkind, Pissarro and Cézanne—was James McNeill Whistler. Whistler, also strongly under the spell of Japanese colour prints, is far more important as an etcher, where his Thames set, published in 1871, and his Venetian set (1880–6) made him world famous. In 1878–9 he did about a dozen lithographs, of which his litho-tints in tender layers of ink, scenes by the river showing the misty atmosphere (Plate 73), are his best. Towards the end of the century he returned to work on the stone, producing about another one hundred and fifty prints, mostly by using transfer-paper, where he restricted himself to a few lines in rather a sketchy manner. This limitation often goes too far, and the results became rather feeble, with the exception of some nudes (Plate 74).

His one-time friend, Walter Richard Sickert, who painted in Impressionistic technique, but with sound pictorial construction, was an excellent draughtsman, and it can only be regretted that he did less than half a dozen lithographs. He was greatly influenced by Degas, whom he had met in Paris in 1883 and who remained his friend. "The Cat's Cradle" (Plate 76) is an early specimen of Sickert as a lithographer. Plate 77 was done in 1907 for the *Neolith*, when a revival of lithography in England was attempted in vain. Sickert took the view that a lithograph done from transfer-paper was not a 'true lithograph", and he attacked Joseph Pennell in the *Saturday Review* for using this method, which Whistler also applied. Pennell brought an action in the High Court against Sickert and the editor of the *Review*, which he naturally won, as Sickert's arguments had no substance.

Wilson Steer, Sickert's fellow-member of the New English Art Club, did a few lithos of lesser importance (Plate 75). Steer, a painter influenced by Constable and the Impressionists, was highly honoured during his lifetime, while Sickert remained a fighter.

Other painters who did their best to revive lithography in Britain are the French Legros, who had settled in England, William Strang, Rothenstein, Ricketts, Brangwyn, Shannon, Conder, Ethel Gabain, Jackson, and the Americans Sargent and Joseph Pennell. The Senefelder Club was founded in 1909 and lithograph classes were started at the County Council Schools. However, masterpieces from great artists were not forthcoming as they were in France, and most prints done during this period of "revival" are forgotten today. Only Augustus John, who also created a name for himself outside the British Isles, did a few drawings of some quality for the stone (Plate 78).

The great success of lithography in France in the 'nineties left its mark in Germany, where this art had fallen into oblivion since Menzel. The foundation of the important German art magazine *Pan* in Berlin in 1895, which contained original graphic work, stimulated German artists to take an interest again in the art which had its origin in Germany. Even French painters like Toulouse-Lautrec, Signac,

Vuillard and Luce contributed original lithographs to this new publication, including one of Lautrec's finest pieces, "Marcelle Lender en buste", printed in eight colours in 1895 (Plate 59).

In South Germany Hans Thoma, son of a peasant from the Black Forest, who had studied in Paris under Couture, and was originally strongly influenced by Courbet, lithographed from 1892 onwards. At this time he was already over fifty years old. Most of his lithographs are made from several stones, and he tried out new materials and new methods (Plate 79). One of these, 'Algraphy', was introduced by a Mr Scholz from Mayence in 1897, adopting aluminium as the best substitute for stone. Thoma's later work suffers from sacrificing artistic quality for a story-telling content.

In Berlin Max Liebermann, often called the German Impressionist, lithographed for *Pan* from 1896. Though he never grasped French Impressionism in painting, he made good use of it in his graphic work. In later years he also illustrated books using this technique, among them Heinrich v. Kleist's *Kleine Schriften*, published by Cassirer in 1917 (Plate 80).

The actual reviver of lithography in Germany was, however, Max Slevogt. Supported by Bruno Cassirer, the publisher, he became a book illustrator on a large scale, with his lithographs for *Sindbad the Sailor*, James Fenimore Cooper's *Story of Leatherstocking*, *The Island of Wak-Wak* (Plate 81), *Benvenuto Cellini*, and others. He was a master-draughtsman who managed to elicit all the secrets from the soft chalk and the brush.

Käthe Kollwitz, best known for her etchings of "Rising of the Weavers", "Carmagnole", and "Death, Mother and Child", also did a number of lithos (Plate 83).

Lovis Corinth, probably the most important artist of his time in Germany, used the stone only in later years when, as a painter, he had found his own style. His form, often baroque, is full of force without being forceful, and the stroke of his chalk resembles that of his brush, revealing great speed without being sketchy (Plate 82). Corinth was somewhat robust by nature, which shows itself also in his art.

German art in the second half of the nineteenth century had no defined tradition. There was the rationalist Menzel, story-telling romanticists like Schwind and Richter, the idealist Feuerbach, who painted theatrical scenes in all their unreality, there was the unique genius of Hans v. Marées and the Swiss Böcklin, but no development based on succession.

Before discussing the various groups of younger painters who changed the entire outlook of art in Germany before 1914, the Norwegian painter Edvard Munch must be mentioned, since his work exercised a decisive influence on Central European art. During the two periods of his stay in Paris, from 1889–92 and from 1895–7, Munch had not only acquainted himself with the art of Pissarro, Seurat, Signac and Van Gogh, but also with Gauguin's woodcuts in colour and in black-and-white. This induced him to continue on similar lines, at least as far as the technique was concerned. In his painting he sometimes faced the dilemma of developing linear values at the expense of tone. This may have persuaded him to express himself to such a great extent through the medium of graphic art, where lithography dominated in the end.

Munch's whole life was influenced by the sad impressions he had in his youth, when Death called several times at his paternal home. His secret fear of "the coming into existence—to be—and to pass away", did not only appear in his "mood of life" but also in his art, his paintings and his graphic work. Though the theme of his work is never purely realistic, he is never literary or a story-teller (Plates 84 and 84a).

He was also a great portraitist, both with brush and on stone. His entire graphic output numbers several hundred pieces, from 1894 until his death in 1944 (Plate 85).

Munch met his first success in Germany, where he lived for many years, and found followers and admirers in the members of "Die Brücke", a group started in 1903 in Dresden, and later in Berlin. The members of this circle of Expressionists were Emil Nolde, Erich Heckel, Ernst Ludwig Kirchner, Max Pechstein and Karl Schmidt-Rottluff.

All the artists of the "Brücke" took great interest in graphic work and lithographed, as their work as painters was already closer to colour woodcut and lithography than at any other period.

Emil Nolde, now eighty-six and the "doyen of painters", practised woodcut, etching and lithography, producing altogether over two hundred prints. As a painter he saw the world in glowing colours, and it was colour which inspired him to do his series of colour-lithographs working direct on the stones, taking many impressions of variation, changing and adding colour, as in "The Three Wise

84A.   EDVARD MUNCH, "TINGEL-TANGEL", LITHOGRAPH, 1895.

Men", "Dancer", "Young Couple", and in later years "Fable Animals" (Plate 88) and "Old Gentle-men".

Ernst Ludwig Kirchner's graphic work consists of landscapes, portraits and themes from the Swiss mountains, where he spent the last years of his life (Plate 90).

Thanks to publishers like Cassirer, Gurlitt, Piper, the Marées Society and others, who commissioned artists to illustrate with original graphic work and who published portfolios of series of original litho-graphs, this art was practised by nearly all painters of note. Besides those already mentioned there were Hofer, Otto Müller, Barlach, Kubin, Otto Dix and Max Beckmann (Plate 93).

A remarkable enterprise was Paul Cassirer's publication of the *Bildermann,* an illustrated paper printed entirely in lithography, appearing twice monthly in 1916, with original work by artists like Kirchner, Heckel, Barlach and Oskar Kokoschka.

Kokoschka's work had great influence on Central European art. In 1918 Paul Westheim[1] assessed Kokoschka's position in relation to the Expressionist movement in general:

"The art of Kokoschka stands beside the manifestations of expressionism as perhaps Cézanne stood beside the companions of his years: beside Manet, Renoir, Degas and Van Gogh. One respects his struggle, but one has nothing in common with his aims."

Kokoschka's lithographic work is very extensive: portfolios like "Bachkantate", "Der gefesselte Kolumbus", "Passion", "Hiob" (Plate 87). As a born portrait painter, he lithographed many portraits, all before 1918. The colour plate, No. 86, "Fox and Grapes", was done in 1952.

[1] Paul Westheim, *Oskar Kokoschka,* Berlin 1918 (Author's translation).

XXXIII

In 1911, inspired by the discoveries of the Cubists in Paris, several artists founded in Munich a kind of group named the "Blaue Reiter"; foremost among its members were Wassilij Kandinsky, Paul Klee, Franz Marc and Alexei v. Jawlensky. Russian-born Kandinsky, the actual leader and older than his friends, had already written his book *The Art of Spiritual Harmony*[1] in 1910; it was published by Piper in Munich in January 1912, second and third impressions following within six months. He was also the first painter to arrive at pure abstraction (1910). He was a great thinker and theorist, Professor at the Bauhaus from 1922 together with Klee, and it was there that he wrote another important book in 1923–6, *Punkt und Linie zu Fläche*.[2] In a special chapter of this book on graphic art he deals with lithography:

"Lithography—of all graphic methods the one invented last—offers the greatest flexibility and elasticity in its manipulation.

The great speed by which it can be performed corresponds completely with the 'spirit of our time', offering at the same time an indestructible solidity of the plate. Point, line and plane, black-and-white and colour—all this can be reached with greatest economy.

The flexibility in the treatment of the stone, which means the easy laying on with any tool and the nearly unlimited possibility of making corrections—especially the removal of faults which neither woodcut nor etching like to endure very much—such resulting in the possibility of starting without absolutely defined plans (for instance, when experimenting), corresponds to the highest degree with the necessity of today, not only the external, but also the internal" (Plate 89).

As compared with Kandinsky the German artist Paul Klee was not an abstract painter. He was a graphic artist by nature, endowed with great inventiveness and a rich inner life of his own. The strong inclination he had for etching and lithography influenced his painting in style and technique (Plates 91 and 92). At the age of forty-one he was invited by Gropius to become a professor at the Bauhaus and later at Weimar, together with Kandinsky and the American Feininger. Klee's lithographs are among the treasures of every collection.

While all this was happening in Germany a new generation was coming to the forefront in France, and new names were making history: Matisse, Picasso, Braque and, soon afterwards, Léger and Juan Gris.

A group of young painters, under the leadership of Henri Matisse, who had outgrown the Post-Impressionism of Bonnard and Vuillard, "rendered light by colour" and organized their pictures in a pleasing way. They held their first exhibition at the Salon d'Automne in 1905 (Matisse, Derain, Vlaminck, Rouault, Marquet, van Dongen, Mangin), which earned them the name of the "Fauves" (wild beasts).

During the fifty years which have passed since then, Matisse has proved that he is not only one of the great painters of the century, but that he is to the same extent a master of drawing. As such he has taken an active part in keeping the graphic arts alive, mainly lithography—his prints number several hundred.

Some show only the outline of his models in his sensitive and characteristic line, others have decorative elements introduced (Plates 94 and 95). Again, another series is designed with all tonal qualities and colour from deepest black to brilliant white (Plate 96). It must be regretted, however, that he has never done any lithography in colour, though some of his compositions cut out in coloured paper have been reproduced by lithographic technique. As an illustrator of books he is rivalled only by Picasso.

Cubism, the inheritance of Cézanne, first practised by Picasso and Braque and soon afterwards by Gris and Léger, revolutionized the arts, lithography also coming under its influence.

Picasso, easily the most fertile of all graphic artists of our time, did not start to lithograph until 1919. He started etching in 1904, and between 1911 and 1914 did etchings in Cubist style. After initial attempts he lithographed four scenes with nudes on the beach, which were published in fifty copies. His first series published by Gallerie Simon in Paris (Henri Kahnweiler) in 1923, was designed in a more elegant classical style, after his somewhat colossal figures of the neo-classical phase (Plate 106). During his first

[1] Kandinsky, *Über das Geistige in der Kunst*, Munich 1912.
[2] Kandinsky, *Punkt und Linie zu Fläche*, Munich 1926 (Author's translation).

phase of lithography, which ended in 1930, he did only one stone, an interior, in his further-developed Cubistic manner, identical with the style of his paintings (Plate 107). His last lithograph, executed in 1930, again shows Picasso in a different mood, and again classical influence makes itself felt as in the thirty etchings of the same period he did for Ovid's *Metamorphosis* (Skira) (Plate 108). From then onwards for over fifteen years he did not touch the stone.

Towards the end of 1945 Picasso started to lithograph in earnest, which meant that lithography became one of his main occupations, and between 1945 and the spring of 1949 he did about one hundred and eighty prints, now catalogued by Mourlot in two large volumes (Plate 109). Since then he has continued and has experimented with all technical possibilities of this art.

In comparison with Picasso, Braque's lithographic output is small in number. His early stone "Still Life" was done in 1921 for Galerie Simon (Plate 104), and is a good example of his late Cubistic period, when some of his subjects retained their natural appearance.

In recent years he has done a number of colour lithographs, still-lifes and classical designs. These lithos do not only show Braque's great graphic abilities but also show what a master of colour this great contemporary painter is (Plate 105).

Though he possesses great feeling for graphic art, Fernand Léger's lithographs and lithographic illustrations have become more numerous only in recent years. Most of them are in colour, with flat surfaces, unmistakably the Léger known from his oils (Plate 117).

Juan Gris, one of the early Cubists, besides doing six lithographed portraits, has illustrated some books for Gallerie Simon in the same medium. Gris' absolute clearness of design, strong architectural composition, feeling for space and for relationship of black and white, indicated further masterpieces would have come from his hand save for his premature death (Plate 103).

Georges Rouault occupies a solitary position in French art. It would be wrong to call him an Expressionist, though his choice of colour is sometimes purely expressive. His graphic work is considerable, etching and aquatint, often in colour, being his favourite media. His lithographs of acrobats and boxers, and his portraits, are mostly executed in wash or tint with scraping (Plate 110). His remarkable self-portrait is sometimes printed in colour, but is just as expressive in black-and-white.

The painters who originally started as 'Fauves' nearly fifty years ago have all gone their own way as time has passed on. Derain absorbed the influence of Cubism and Picasso (Plate 99); Dufy (Plate 102), after a phase of close relationship to Cézanne, developed his own original handwriting; Vlaminck (Plate 97), at one time flirting with Cubism, arrived at landscapes in intense colour, somewhat related to a moderated Expressionism.

Maurice Utrillo preferred—and still paints and draws—'landscapes' of Paris buildings, boulevards and suburbs, in his own peculiar style (Plate 98).

Jacques Villon, influenced in his youth by Lautrec's colour lithos, has become a Neo-Cubist.

Russian-born Marc Chagall, an original artist of high qualities and friend of Apollinaire in 1910 when he came to Paris, can be regarded as instigator of modern Surrealism. He is a poet at heart, and his work, in glowing colours and forms of his own invention, has a fantastic and dream-like quality, without being literary. His graphic work is extensive and, especially in recent years, he has occupied himself with colour lithography. He has illustrated *Arabian Nights* in this technique, using strong but sensitively chosen tints of great variation. These, and other colour lithos he did recently, are among the best done in polychrome (Plates 100 and 101).

German-born Max Ernst (Plate 111), who together with Hans Arp and Picabia went through the 'Dada' movement, is the foremost exponent of modern Surrealism, also documented by Salvador Dali and Tanguy. Masson, originally belonging to this movement, went beyond its dogma (Plate 112), as did de Chirico (Plate 114), who in recent years denounced his earlier work.

Joan Miro who, indebted to Klee, has invented his own new language of signs and splendid colour, is also a great graphic artist. His art lends itself most excellently to its expression in lithographic technique (Plate 118).

In Italy Severini, Massimo Campigli (Plate 115), the sculptor Marini (Plate 113) and a number of younger painters joined the ever-growing movement of those who preferred the stone, a movement which started with Lautrec and the 'Nabis' and continues to the present day. The publication of luxury editions of classical and modern literature illustrated with original lithographs, portfolios and limited editions of single prints was started by Vollard. This was taken up by other art dealers and publishers, like Kahnweiler (first Galerie Simon, later Galerie Louise Leiris), Skira, Tériade (the publisher of *Verve*), Fabiani, Au sans Pareil, Bordas, La Sirène and others; followed, after the war, by Maeght with his *Pierre à Feu* publications and *Derrière le Miroir*, to which artists like Braque, Chagall, Léger, Matisse, Miro and the Swiss sculptor Giacometti (Plate 116) contributed. All this provided a sound basis for this art. *La Guilde Internationale de la Gravure* in Geneva published colour lithos by Lurcat, Goerg, Amiet, Erni, Laurens, Villon, Hayter, Clavé, Lhote, Pignon, Severini and by many of the younger painters and sculptors at a moderate price, and in doing so popularised the print in France and Switzerland (Plates 113 and 115).

★

The modern trend in art as started by the Cubists had a certain influence in England, where Wyndham Lewis, Edward Wadsworth and the sculptors Gaudier-Brzeska and Jacob Epstein tried to reform the official conception of art.

Paul Nash, an official war artist (1914–18), did a series of lithographs (Plate 119), and it is a matter of regret that in his later years he hardly ever touched the stone.

Frances Hodgkins, the woman artist from New Zealand, lithographed only once (Plate 120), and Barnett Freedman illustrated some books.

But there was nothing like the great revival of lithography in France and Germany, nor was the artist-illustrated book cultivated in England as it was in France.

Finally, in 1948, Rex Nan Kivell (Redfern Gallery), together with Mrs Stamper and Miss Lucas, founded the Society of London Painter-Printers, who held their first exhibition at the Redfern Gallery the same year. Well over fifty painters contributed colour lithographs, to mention only a few names: Graham Sutherland, John Piper, Robert Colquhoun, James MacBride, Matthew Smith, Duncan Grant, Vanessa Bell, Caroline Lucas, Prunella Clough, William Scott, John Minton, Victor Pasmore, Ceri Richards and Jankel Adler. To many of these painters lithography was then a new process, while others, like Piper or Colquhoun, who had lithographed before, or Graham Sutherland, whose graphic work was already considerable, found no difficulties in this technique, except the printing. Since the days of Whistler and Way, English printers have lacked experience and trained personnel, and today there is no one comparable to Mourlot in Paris.

Graham Sutherland, the leading figure of international reputation in modern British painting, is an experienced graphic artist, who not only knows how to explore the technical possibilities of the stone, but whose work is that of an original artist who transmits his idiom by means of a powerful language of expression and feeling for form and space, supported by a rich and sensitive colour (Plates 122 and 123).

Though an outstanding draughtsman, Henry Moore, the great sculptor, has done only a very limited number of lithographs (Plate 121).

Since the enterprise of Rex Nan Kivell in 1948 many more young painters in Britain have tried their hand at lithography; there has even been an exhibition of 'Coronation Lithographs' at the Royal College of Art. Out of these Leonard Rosoman and Edward Bawden will be remembered.

Today, one hundred and fifty years after the first artists' lithographs were published, this minor art has established itself not only with the artists themselves but also with the public, who, in increasing numbers, take an interest in collecting these works from the past and the present, for their aesthetic enjoyment, assembling at the same time a history of the arts *en miniature* in their own homes—or decorating their walls with the artist's original work at a modest price.[1]

[1] Interesting figures about the revaluation of artists' lithographs are given in Section C under Notes on Artists. *See especially* Toulouse-Lautrec, Signac, Bonnard, and Manet.

The reproduction of the watermark "Whatman 1820" (see page xxii), was made after an original impression of Ingres's four portraits on one sheet, in the possession of Messrs P. & D. Colnaghi & Co. Ltd, London.

SECTION B

He is not here: for he is risen. &c.

1. BENJAMIN WEST, "THE ANGEL". POLYAUTOGRAPH, DEL. 1801, FIRST PUBL. 1803

2.   THOMAS STOTHARD, "THE LOST APPLE". POLYAUTOGRAPH, N.D., FIRST PUBL. 1803

3. HENRY FUSELI, "O EVENING THOU BRINGEST ALL". POLYAUTOGRAPH, N.D., PUBL. 1803

4. PETER BAILEY, "BANDITS". POLYAUTOGRAPH, DEL. 1802, UNPUBLISHED

5. H. BERNARD CHALON, "HORSES". POLYAUTOGRAPH IN CHALK MANNER, DEL. 1804

6. RICHARD COOPER, "LANDSCAPE WITH BOATS". POLYAUTOGRAPH, DEL. AND PUBL. 1806

7. HENRY FUSELI, "THE RAPE OF GANYMED". POLYAUTOGRAPH, N.D., DEL. ABOUT 1806

8. WILHELM REUTER, "NYMPH BATHING". POLYAUTOGRAPH. DEL. AND PUBL. 1805

Polyautographische Zeichnung von G. Schadow.

9. JOH. G. SCHADOW, "ORESTES AND THE EUMENIDES". POLYAUTOGRAPH, PUBL. 1804

10. JOH. G. SCHADOW, "COUNCILLOR SIEGMUND WILH. WOHLBRÜCK". ORIG. LITHOGRAPH, 1822

Versuch die lieblische schmerzvolle Wehmuth auszudrucken welche das Herz beim Klange des Gottesdienstes aus der Kirche herschallend erfüllt. auf Stein gezeichnet von Schinkel.

11. KARL FRIEDRICH SCHINKEL, "GOTHIC CHURCH". ORIG. LITHOGRAPH, N.D., PUBL. 1810

KATHERINE ANNE (NORTH) LADY GLENBERVIE.
Nat. 16 Feb. 1760. Mort. 6 Feb. 1817.

SYLVESTER (DOUGLAS) LORD GLENBERVIE.
Nat. 18 May O.S. 1744.

THE HONᵇˡᵉ FREDERIC SYLVESTER DOUGLAS.
Nat. 8 Feb. 1791. Mort. 21 Oct. 1819.

FREDERIC (NORTH) EARL OF GUILDFORD.
Nat. 7 Feb. 1766.

12.   JEAN DOMINIQUE INGRES, "FOUR PORTRAITS ON ONE STONE". ORIG. LITHOGRAPH, DEL. 1815

13.   PIERRE NARCISSE GUÉRIN, "THE IDLER".   ORIG. LITHOGRAPH, 1816–17

14.   BARON VIVAN DENON, "DENON, MAKING A DRAWING OF FRIENDS". ORIG. LITHOGRAPH, 1816

en 10 minutes. *K. Vernet 1817*

15. HORACE VERNET, "GRENADIER OF WATERLOO". ORIG. LITHOGRAPH, "IN TEN MINUTES", 1817

16.   BARON ANTOINE-JEAN GROS, "CHIEF OF THE MAMELUKES".   ORIG. LITHOGRAPH, 1817

17. THÉODORE GÉRICAULT, "MAMELUKE DEFENDING A WOUNDED TRUMPETER". ORIG. LITHOGRAPH, 1818

HORSES EXERCISING

THE FLEMISH FARRIER

18.   THÉODORE GÉRICAULT, "HORSES EXERCISING".   ORIG. LITH. DEL. AND PUBL. IN ENGLAND, 1821

19.   THÉODORE GÉRICAULT, "THE FLEMISH FARRIER".   ORIG. LITH. DEL. AND PUBL. IN ENGLAND, 1821

20.   NICOLAS-TOUSSAINT CHARLET, "THE FRENCH SOLDIER". ORIG. LITHOGRAPH, 1818

Une Lecture.

Prud'hon inv. et del.   Litho. de l'Motte.

21.   PIERRE PAUL PRUD'HON, "READING". ORIG. LITHOGRAPH, 1822

22. ALEXANDER ORLOWSKI, "SLEDGE RIDE IN RUSSIA". ORIG. LITHOGRAPH, DEL. 1820

23. ALEXANDER ORLOWSKI, "ON THE PERSIAN BORDER". ORIG. LITHOGRAPH, DEL. 1819

24. JAMES WARD, "ADONIS", A CELEBRATED HORSE. ORIG. LITHOGRAPH, DEL. AND PUBL. 1824

25. DAVID OCTAVIUS HILL, "LANDSCAPE IN PERTHSHIRE". ORIG. LITHOGRAPH, 1821

26.   THOMAS BEWICK, "THE CADGER'S TROT".   FIRST STATE, ORIG. LITHOGRAPH, 1821

27.   THOMAS BEWICK, "THE CADGER'S TROT".   SECOND STATE, SEE NOTES PART C

28. RICHARD PARKES BONINGTON, "RUE DU GROS HORLOGE, ROUEN". ORIG. LITHOGRAPH, 1824

29. FRANCISCO DE GOYA, "THE BULLS OF BORDEAUX". PLATE 4. ORIG. LITHOGRAPH, 1825

30. FRANCISCO DE GOYA, "SPANISH DANCE". ORIG. LITHOGRAPH, 1825

31. FRANCISCO DE GOYA, "THE BULLS OF BORDEAUX", PLATE 3. ORIG. LITHOGRAPH, 1825

32. FRANCISCO DE GOYA, "THE DUEL". ORIG. LITHOGRAPH, DATE DISPUTED, 1819–25

33. EUGÈNE DELACROIX, "FAUST AND MEPHISTOPHELES DURING THE NIGHT OF THE SABBATH". 1828

34. EUGÈNE DELACROIX, "SHEET WITH TWELVE ANTIQUE MEDALS". ORIG. LITH., DEL. 1825, PUBL. 1864

35. EUGÈNE DELACROIX, "YOUNG TIGER PLAYING WITH HIS MOTHER". ORIG. LITHOGRAPH, 1831

36. ANTOINE-LOUIS BARYE, "LIONESS PLAYING WITH HER LITTLE ONES". ORIG. LITHOGRAPH, 1832

37. ACHILLE DEVERIA, "ALEXANDRE DUMAS, PÈRE". ORIG. LITHOGRAPH, 1829

38. EUGÈNE ISABEY, "INTERIOR OF A PORT". ORIG. LITHOGRAPH, 1833

39. PAUL HUET, "THE HILLS OF ST SAUVEUR, NEAR ROUEN". ORIG. LITHOGRAPH, 1831

40. JULES DUPRÉ, "PASTURE LAND NEAR LIMOGES". ORIG. LITHOGRAPH, 1835

41. THÉODORE CHASSÉRIAU, "APOLLO AND DAPHNE". ORIG. LITHOGRAPH, 1844

42. N. V. DIAZ, "THE FOOLISH LOVERS". ORIG. LITHOGRAPH, 1849

43.   HONORÉ DAUMIER, "GUIZOT".   ORIG. LITHOGRAPH, 1833

44.   HONORÉ DAUMIER, "THE WOBBLING HEAD".   ORIG. LITHOGRAPH, 1834

45. HONORÉ DAUMIER, "THIS HAS KILLED THAT". ORIG. LITHOGRAPH, 1871

46. PAUL GAVARNI, "THE BEAU OF THE DÉBUTANTE". ORIG. LITHOGRAPH, 1852

47. ADOLF V. MENZEL, "THE BEAR PIT". ORIG. LITHOGRAPH, 1851.

48. EDOUARD MANET, "THE BARRICADE". ORIG. LITHOGRAPH, 1871, BEFORE LETTER

49. EDOUARD MANET, "AT THE WINDOW". ORIG. LITHOGRAPH FROM THE "RAVEN", 1875.

50. CAMILLE COROT, "REMINISCENCE OF ITALY". ORIG. LITHOGRAPH, 1871.

51. HENRI FANTIN-LATOUR, "SARAH THE BATHER". ORIG. LITHOGRAPH, 1892.

52. ODILON REDON, "HEAD OF CHRIST". ORIG. LITHOGRAPH, 1887

53.   ODILON REDON, "THE JUROR".   ORIG. LITHOGRAPHIC ILLUSTRATION FOR A DRAMA, 1887

54. EUGÈNE CARRIÈRE, "MARGUERITE CARRIÈRE". ORIG. LITHOGRAPH FROM TWO STONES, 1901

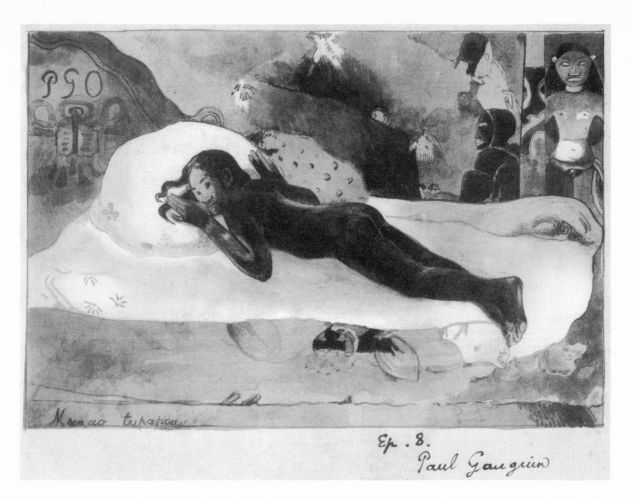

55. PAUL GAUGUIN, "MANAO TUPAPAU"   ORIG. LITHOGRAPH, 1894, INCLUDED IN "NOA NOA"

56. PAUL GAUGUIN, "WOMEN FROM BRITTANY", ORIG. LITHOGRAPH ON ZINC, 1889

57.   HENRI DE TOULOUSE-LAUTREC, "LA GOULUE AND VALENTIN". ORIG. LITHOGRAPH, 1894

58. TOULOUSE-LAUTREC, "LA GOULUE AND HER SISTER". ORIG. LITHOGRAPH IN COLOUR, 1892

59. TOULOUSE-LAUTREC, "MISS LENDER, HALF-LENGTH PORTRAIT". ORIG. LITHO IN EIGHT COLOURS, 1895

60. EDGAR DEGAS, "AFTER THE BATH". ORIG. LITHOGRAPH, 1895, FIRST PLATE

61. PAUL CÉZANNE, "PORTRAIT OF CÉZANNE". ORIG. LITHOGRAPH, 1898

No 69
P. Signac

62. PAUL SIGNAC, "THE PORT OF ST TROPEZ". ORIG. LITHOGRAPH IN COLOUR, 1898

Ep d'etat n° 8

Baigneuses à l'ombre des bois boisés

63. CAMILLE PISSARRO, "BATHERS IN THE SHADE OF A WOOD". ORIG. LITHOGRAPH ON ZINC, 1895

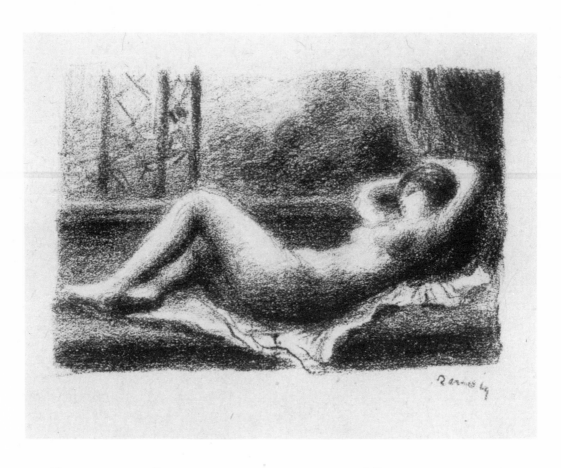

64.   ALFRED SISLEY, "THE BANK OF THE LOING NEAR ST MAMMÈS".   ORIG. LITHOGRAPH, 1896

65.   AUGUSTE RENOIR, "ODALISQUE".   ORIG. LITHOGRAPH, 1904

66. AUGUSTE RENOIR, "PORTRAIT OF RICHARD WAGNER". ORIG. LITHOGRAPH ABOUT 1900

67. PIERRE BONNARD, "MUNICIPAL GUARD". ORIG. LITHOGRAPH, 1893

68. PIERRE BONNARD, "THE BOULEVARDS". ORIG. LITHOGRAPH IN COLOUR, 1899

69. PIERRE BONNARD, "WOMAN SITTING IN HER BATH". ORIG. LITHOGRAPH IN NINE COLOURS, 1942

70.   EDOUARD VUILLARD, "YOUNG WOMAN, LEANING ON HER ELBOW".   ORIG. LITHOGRAPH, 1899

71.   EDOUARD VUILLARD, "INTERIOR, OF THE HANGING–LAMP PERIOD".   ORIG. LITHO. IN FIVE COLOURS, 1899

72. MAURICE DENIS, "MOTHER AND CHILD". ORIG. LITHOGRAPH PRINTED IN GREY, 1897

73.   JAMES MCNEILL WHISTLER, "EARLY MORNING". ORIG. LITHOGR. 1879

74.   JAMES MCNEILL WHISTLER, "NUDE MODEL RECLINING". ORIG. LITHOGRAPH, 1893

75. PHILIP WILSON STEER, "THE NURSEMAID". ORIG. LITHOGRAPH, 1892

76. WALTER RICHARD SICKERT, "CAT'S CRADLE". ORIG. LITHOGRAPH, 1892

77.   WALTER RICHARD SICKERT, "WOMAN WITH HAT". ORIG. LITHOGRAPH, 1907

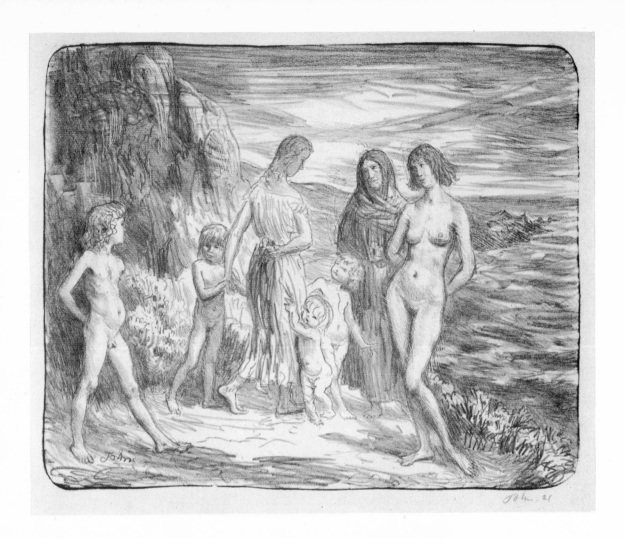

78. AUGUSTUS JOHN, "THE BATHERS". ORIG. LITHOGRAPH, 1921

79. HANS THOMA, "PORTRAIT OF HANS THOMA". ORIG. LITHOGRAPH FROM THREE STONES, 1894

80. MAX LIEBERMANN, "ILLUSTRATION TO HEINRICH V. KLEIST". ORIG. LITHOGRAPH, 1917

81. MAX SLEVOGT, "THE ISLANDS OF WAK WAK". ILLUSTRATIONS IN LITHOGRAPHY, 1922

82. LOVIS CORINTH, "THE CREATION OF ADAM". ORIG. LITHOGRAPH IN COLOUR, 1923

83. KÄTHE KOLLWITZ, "PORTRAIT OF THE ARTIST". ORIG. LITHOGRAPH, 1920

84.   EDVARD MUNCH, "THE SCREAM".   ORIG. LITHOGRAPH, 1895

85. EDVARD MUNCH, "PORTRAIT OF WOMAN WITH BLACK SCARF". ORIG. LITHOGRAPH, 1920

86.   OSKAR KOKOSCHKA, "THE FOX AND THE GRAPES". ORIG. LITHOGRAPH IN COLOUR, 1952

87. OSKAR KOKOSCHKA, "HIOB". A DRAMA BY KOKOSCHKA ILLUSTRATED WITH ORIG. LITHOGRAPHS, 1918

88.   EMIL NOLDE, "FABULOUS ANIMALS".   ORIG. LITHOGRAPH IN COLOUR, 1926

89.   WASSILY KANDINSKY, "COMPOSITION WITH BLUE TRIANGLE". ORIG. LITHOGRAPH IN COLOUR, 1922

E. L. Kirchner

Bildnis Carl Sternheim

90.   ERNST LUDWIG KIRCHNER, "PORTRAIT OF CARL STERNHEIM".   ORIG. LITHOGRAPH, 1916

91. PAUL KLEE, "THE WITCH WITH THE COMB". ORIG. LITHOGRAPH, 1922

92.   PAUL KLEE, "IN THE SPIRIT OF HOFFMANN".   ORIG. LITHOGRAPH IN COLOUR, 1921

93. MAX BECKMANN, "CLOWN AND MASK". ORIG. LITHOGRAPH, 1920

94.   HENRI MATISSE, "BALLET DANCER RECUMBENT". ORIG. LITHOGRAPH ABOUT 1928

95.   HENRI MATISSE, "NUDE". ORIG. LITHOGRAPH, 1926

96.   HENRI MATISSE, "PERSIAN".   ORIG. LITHOGRAPH, 1929

97. MAURICE DE VLAMINCK, "THE BRIDGE NEAR CHATON". ORIG. LITHOGRAPH IN COLOUR, ABOUT 1927

98. MAURICE UTRILLO, "MONTMARTRE". ORIG. LITHOGRAPH, 1943

99.   ANDRÉ DERAIN, "FACE".   ORIG. LITHOGRAPH, ABOUT 1925

100.   MARC CHAGALL, "THE PAINTER AND HIS MODEL". ORIG. LITHOGRAPH, 1952

101. MARC CHAGALL, "VISION OF PARIS". ORIG. LITHOGRAPH IN COLOUR, 1952

102. RAOUL DUFY, "THE BATHER", LARGE PLATE. ORIG. LITHOGRAPH IN COLOUR, ABOUT 1927

103. JUAN GRIS, "LACARTELETTRE". ORIG. LITHOGRAPH FOR "DON'T CUT OFF, MISS", 1921

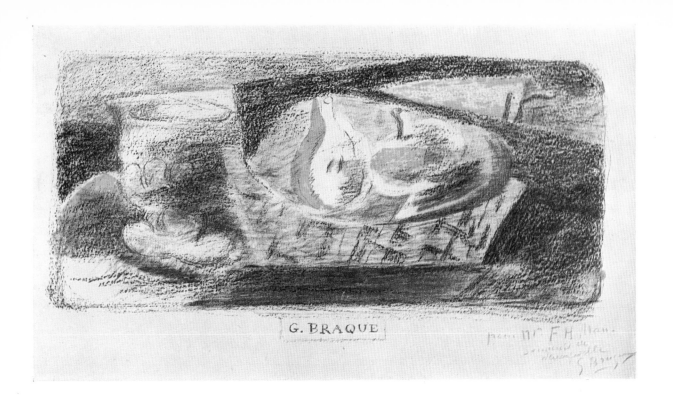

104. GEORGE BRAQUE, "STILL LIFE". ORIG. LITHOGRAPH IN COLOUR, 1921

105. GEORGE BRAQUE, "TEAPOT AND LEMON". ORIG. LITHOGRAPH IN SIX COLOURS, 1947

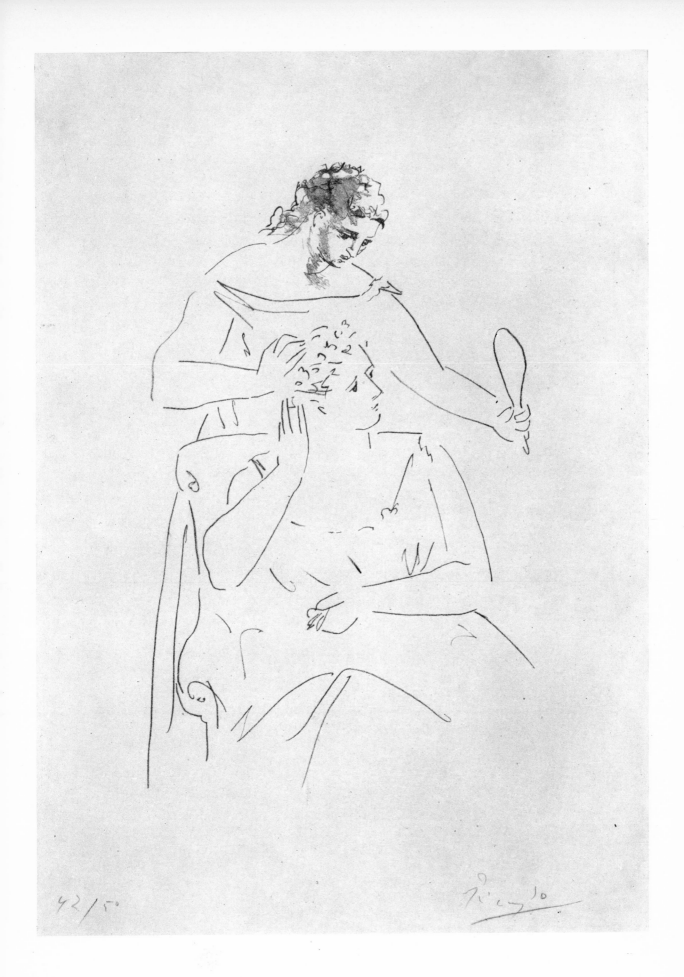

42/50

106. PABLO PICASSO, "THE TOILET". ORIG. LITHOGRAPH, 1923

107. PABLO PICASSO, "INTERIOR". ORIG. LITHOGRAPH, 1926

108. PABLO PICASSO, "THE PAINTER AND HIS MODEL". ORIG. LITHOGRAPH, 1930

109. PABLO PICASSO, "FIGURE WITH STRIPED BODICE". ORIG. LITHOGRAPH IN SIX COLOURS, 1949

110. GEORGE ROUAULT, "CLOWNS". ORIG. LITHOGRAPH, ABOUT 1928

111. MAX ERNST, "COMPOSITION". ORIG. LITHOGRAPH IN COLOUR, 1950

112.   ANDRÉ MASSON, "MATERNITY".   ORIG. LITHOGRAPH, 1951, PRINTED IN GREEN

113.   MARINO MARINI, "HORSES".   ORIG. LITHOGRAPH IN THREE COLOURS, 1952

114.   GIORGIO DE CHIRICO, "GLADIATOR". ORIG. LITHOGRAPH WITH COLOUR, 1929

115.   MASSIMO CAMPIGLI, "THE NECKLACE". ORIG. LITHOGRAPH IN COLOUR, 1952

116.   ALBERTO GIACOMETTI, "THE STUDIO".   ORIG. LITHOGRAPH, 1952

117.   FERNAND LÉGER, "COMPOSITION WITH PROFILE".   ORIG. LITHOGRAPH IN FIVE COLOURS, 1948

8/75   Miró.

118.   JOAN MIRO, "COMPOSITION WITH CROSSED BEAMS". ORIG. LITHOGRAPH ABOUT 1949

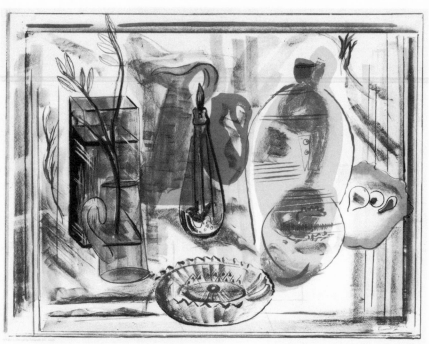

119.   PAUL NASH, "MINE CRATER HILL 60". ORIG. LITHOGRAPH, 1917

120.   FRANCES HODGKINS, "STILL LIFE". ORIG. LITHOGRAPH IN COLOUR, 1938

121. HENRY MOORE, "ILLUSTRATION TO PROMETHEUS". ORIG. LITHOGRAPH IN COLOUR, 1950

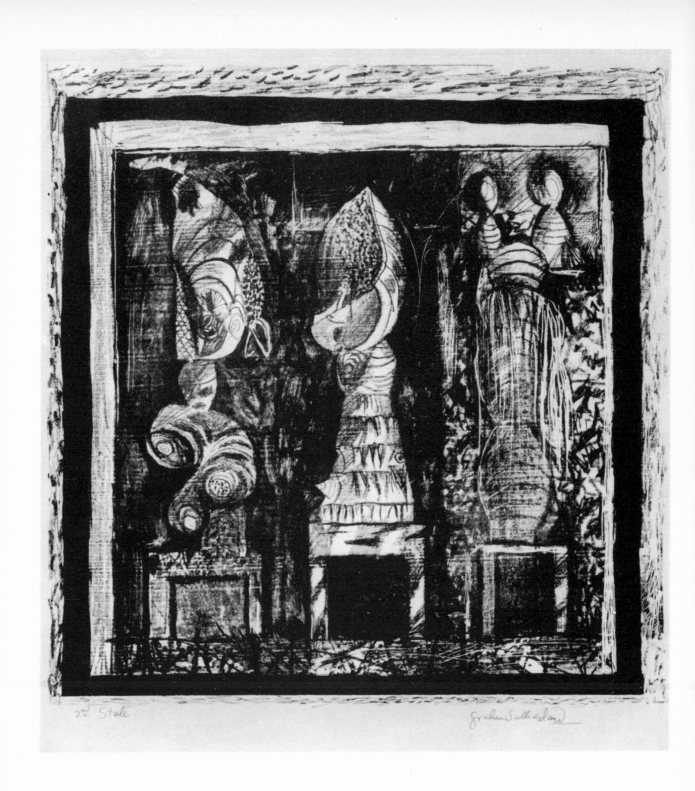

2nd State.

Graham Sutherland

122.   GRAHAM SUTHERLAND, "THREE STANDING FORMS".   ORIG. LITHOGRAPH, 1950

123. GRAHAM SUTHERLAND, "STUDY LA PETITE AFRIQUE". ORIG. LITHOGRAPH, 1953

SECTION C

NOTES ON ARTISTS AND THEIR PRINTS

The numbers refer to the numerals beneath the reproductions of the lithographs

1 WEST, BENJAMIN, P.R.A., 1738–1806. "THE ANGEL", DATED 1801. POLYAUTOGRAPH, 12¾×9 in., published in *Specimens of Polyautography*, 1803, by P. H. André in London, reprinted in 1806 by Vollweiler. British Museum, Print Coll.

This is the first lithograph of artistic merit ever done in any country. West, born at Springfield, Penn., U.S.A., came to London about 1760, after having completed his studies in Italy. He became the second President of the Royal Academy in 1792, succeeding Reynolds. George II patronised him for nearly forty years. His best-known paintings, painted in the official manner of his day, are: "Edward III at Crécy", "The Black Prince", and "Christ healing the Sick". West was buried in St Paul's.

2 STOTHARD, THOMAS, R.A., 1755–1834. "THE LOST APPLE", NO DATE. POLYAUTOGRAPH, 12½×9 in., published in *Specimens of Polyautography*, 1803, by P. H. André, reprinted by Vollweiler in 1806. Author's Coll.

Stothard, mainly known through his designs, of which about 300 were engraved (Boydell's *Shakespeare*, *The Pilgrim's Progress*, *Canterbury Tales*), became R.A. in 1794 and Academy librarian in 1813. At one time friend of Blake, who had to do engravings after Stothard's design. After Blake's estrangement from Stothard, Blake complained "of his mechanical employment as an engraver to a fellow designer who first borrowed from one, that, in his servile capacity, had to copy that comrade's version of his own invention" (Gilchrist, *William Blake*).

2a WEST, RAPHAEL LAMAR, 1769–1850. "STUDY OF A TREE", DATED 1802. POLYAUTOGRAPH, 12¾×9 in., published in 1806 by Vollweiler. Author's Coll.

R. L. West was the son of Benjamin West, P.R.A., and a painter, etcher and lithographer. From 1800–2 he visited the U.S.A. (*see* text, Part A).

3 FUSELI, HENRY, R.A., 1742–1825. "EVENING THOU BRINGEST ALL", NO DATE. POLYAUTOGRAPH, 9×12¾ in., published 1803 by P. H. André in *Specimens of Polyautography*, reprinted 1806 by Vollweiler. British Museum, Print Coll.

Fuseli, Swiss-born from Zürich (original name Johann Heinrich Füssli) became Professor of Paints at the Royal Academy in 1799, and played an important part in London's art life, also as a critic and writer (Winkelmann translation), while his friend Blake remained in the background. However, Fuseli was a genuine admirer of Blake, and he declared "the time would come when the finest would be

as much sought after and treasured . . . as those of Michelangelo now" (Gilchrist, *Blake*). Fuseli was "influenced" by Reynolds and "inspired" by Blake. Of his 200 paintings, "Nightmare" is the best known.

4 BAILEY, P. "BANDITTI", DATED 1802. POLYAUTOGRAPH, 9⅛×12¾ in. Author's Coll., not in the British Museum or Victoria & Albert Museum.

Bailey did two more Polyautographs in 1802, "Lion Asleep", British Museum, and "Œdipus and Antigone", British Museum and Author's Coll.

Little is known about Bailey, catalogued at the British Museum as Peter Bailey. Bénezit mentions Bailey as *paysagiste* showing paintings at the Royal Academy in 1832–3 and at Suffolk Street.

5 CHALON, H. B., 1770–1849. "HORSES" 1804. POLYAUTOGRAPH, 9 × 12¾ in. THE FIRST SUCCESSFUL LITHOGRAPH IN THE CHALK MANNER. Published by Vollweiler in 1806. British Museum, Print Coll.

Chalon, painter and lithographer, was animal painter to the Duchess of York (1796) and from 1820 animal painter to His Majesty George IV. In 1827 he published a work about the horse printed in lithography.

6 COOPER, RICHARD, 1740–1814. "LANDSCAPE WITH BOATS", DATED 1806. POLYAUTOGRAPH IN CHALK, 8¾×12⅝ in. Published by Vollweiler in 1806. British Museum, Print Coll.

Cooper did pen lithographs as early as 1802, one of which was published by André in 1803. Cooper, at one time drawing master at Eton College and to Queen Charlotte, painted landscapes (Windsor and Richmond) and was also an engraver and etcher.

7 FUSELI, HENRY. "TON KAI ANHPEIΨ-ANTO", NO DATE. POLYAUTOGRAPH, *c.* 1806, chalk, 12 3/16×9 5/16 in. Victoria & Albert Museum, Print Coll. (*see also* No. 3).

Lettered in Greek with words from the *Iliad*, book xx.

7a BLAKE, WILLIAM, 1757–1827. "JOB IN PROSPERITY", NO DATE, *c.* 1807. RUSSELL 23. POLYAUTOGRAPH, 8½×12⅛ in. British Museum, Print Coll.

William Blake, engraver, painter, poet, was the outstanding British artist of his time. He exhibited at the Royal Academy from 1780. He invented his own process of engraving, which he used for printing and illustrating his poems and writings: *Songs of Innocence, Songs of Experience,*

America, a prophecy, *Jerusalem*—mostly coloured by his own hand. His twenty-one original engravings to the *Book of Job*, published in 1826, belong to his finest graphic work. His water-colours to Dante and many other figure subjects are priceless. He also did some wood engravings for Thornton's *Virgil*, and engraved after Stothard, Fuseli, Flaxman and others, to earn his living. His paintings (a kind of tempera) include "Canterbury Pilgrims", "The Spiritual Form of Pitt", "Jacob's Dream" and "The Last Judgement". This, his only lithograph, was done about 1807. Blake's graphic work is catalogued by A. G. Russell and by Geoffrey Keynes (*see* text, Part A).

7b BARKER, THOMAS, 1769–1847. KNOWN AS BARKER OF BATH. "RUSTIC FIGURE", 1813, $8\frac{3}{4}\times 6$ in. One of forty original lithographs published by Barker in 1813 in one volume of the same title. Author's Coll.

Barker lithographed from 1803, his "Boy Sitting" being included in André's publication of that year. He painted landscapes, rustic scenes, some of which, especially "The Woodman", became popular. Another publication of landscape lithographs was announced by Barker for 1814 (*see* text, Part A).

8 REUTER, WILHELM, 1768–1834. "BADENDE NYMPHE", DATED 1805. POLYAUTOGRAPH, $16\frac{1}{8}\times 13\frac{3}{4}$ in., published in Reuter's *Polyautographs*, Berlin 1805. Dussler 25A.

Reuter, pioneer of artistic lithography in Germany, published his *Polyautographische Zeichnungen vorzüglicher Berliner Künstler* from 1804 till 1808. They were modelled on the English publication of André. Reuter was a portrait and miniature painter, from 1798 a court painter. He also did commercial graphic and designs. His graphic work is catalogued by Paul Hoffmann.

9 SCHADOW, JOHANN GOTTFRIED, 1764–1850. "ORESTES UND DIE EUMENIDEN", 1804. POLYAUTOGRAPH, $11\frac{1}{2}\times 15\frac{3}{4}$ in., published in Reuter's *Polyautographs*, Berlin 1804. Mackowsky 67.

Schadow, the leading sculptor in Berlin, was under classical influence in his plastic art (Monument of Queen Luise, Quadriga on Brandenburg Tor, Monument for Blücher). He became Director of the Berlin Academy in 1815, and was closely related to the Court of Friedrich Wilhelm IV, who decorated him with the highest Prussian order, "Pour le Mérite". Schadow was the first artist of fame in Germany to take an interest in lithography, which he kept up until his death, executing altogether forty-five lithographs, including some eleven done from zinc. His graphic work is catalogued by H. Mackowsky.

10 SCHADOW, JOH. GOTTFRIED. "KRIEGSRAT SIEGMUND WILH. WOHLBRÜCK", 1822. Original lithograph, $4\frac{1}{8}\times 4$ in., Mackowsky 71, first state, before the artist's signature on the stone. Author's Coll.

10a STRIXNER, JOH. NEPOMUK, 1782–1855. FRONTISPIECE AND PAGE 22 FROM THE "PRAYER BOOK OF EMPEROR MAXIMILIAN". Lithographed by Strixner in 1807, after the original design of Albrecht Dürer, published by Senefelder in 1808. This is the first important book publication in lithography (Dussler I). A second issue (Dussler II) appeared in 1817 in London, *Oratio Dominica*, the plates designed by J. B. Stuntz and Elect Stuntz; some leaves carry the name of Strixner. The first original edition was issued without the text, as reproduced here. Author's Coll. Strixner also reproduced famous paintings from the Galleries in Schleifsheim and Munich together with Piloty, and worked as the first lithographer from two stones (one for tone).

11 SCHINKEL, KARL FRIEDRICH, 1781–1841. "GOTISCHE KIRCHE", 1810, $19\frac{1}{4}\times 13\frac{1}{2}$ in., printed on India paper. Dussler 7. Author's Coll.

Schinkel was the leading architect of the classical period in Prussia (Theatre Royal, Berlin; The New Guard-House, Unter den Linden, Royal Museum). He occupied himself early with lithography. He also did some stage designs for Mozart's *Magic Flute*, and was a painter.

11a QUAGLIO, LORENZ, 1793–1869. "PORTRAIT OF SENEFELDER", 1818 (frontispiece of this book). Dussler III a. 3, $11\frac{1}{4}\times 8\frac{7}{8}$ in. Author's Coll.

Lorenz Quaglio belonged to the famous Quaglio family of architects, painters and engravers, Angelo, Domenico, Simon, Giovanni Maria. Lorenz was also a landscape painter and etcher.

11b BERGERET, PIERRE NOLASQUE, 1782–1863. "ADVERTISEMENT IN PEN LITHOGRAPHY FOR P. ANDRE AND MR BELL IN LONDON, FOR A PUBLICATION BY POLYAUTOGRAPHY OF PARIS ART TREASURES", *c.* 1803. $8\frac{1}{2}\times 12\frac{9}{16}$ in. British Museum, Print Coll. (*see* text, Part A).

Bergeret, pupil of David, a history and genre painter, was the first French artist to explore lithography. The specimen reproduced here and not recorded before, is doubtless one of the very earliest French lithographs.

12 INGRES, JEAN DOMINIQUE, 1781–1867. "FOUR PORTRAITS ON ONE STONE", DATED ROME, 1815, printed by Hullmandel *c.* 1820. Original lithograph, $17\frac{1}{2}\times 12\frac{1}{2}$ in.

Sylvester Douglas, L.D. 2, Katherine Anne, L.D. 3, Frederic North, L.D. 4, Frederic Sylvester, L.D. 5. Printed on one sheet of paper. Author's Coll.

R-R-R, usually only found in cut-up condition. Ingres, pupil of David, worked in Rome 1806–20, where these portraits were drawn by this greatest draughtsman of his time. Some of his best-known paintings are: "L'Odalisque", "Le Bain Turc", "La Source", and portraits of M. Bertin and Mme Rivière. His graphic work is catalogued by L. Delteil.

13 GUÉRIN, PIERRE NARCISSE, 1774–1833. "LE PARESSEUX", 1816–17, Bouchot 7. 10⅝ × 7¾ in. Original lithograph. Author's Coll.

Pupil of Regnault, Guérin was a history painter. His three lithographs, "Le Paresseux", "Le Vigilant" and "Repos du Monde", were done in 1816–17, and belong to the incunabula of French lithography.

14 DENON, VIVAN (BARON), 1747–1833. "DENON DESSINANT DES AMIS", 1816. 5¾ × 7⅝ in. Original lithograph. Author's Coll.

Denon, one of the pioneers of lithography in France, has done a great number of lithographs. During the first Empire he was "Directeur Général des Musées en France".

15 VERNET, HORACE, 1789–1863. "GRENA-DIER DE WATERLOO", 1817. Beraldi 35. 7⅞ × 5¾ in. Original lithograph.

Together with his father Carle, Vernet did a very great number of lithographs. As painters, both showed preference for battle scenes.

16 GROS, ANTOINE-JEAN (BARON), 1771–1835. "CHEF DES MAMELUCKS", 1817, FIRST STATE, before the artist's signature on the stone. 12½ × 9 in. Original lithograph. Author's Coll.

One of the two original lithographs of Gros. Pupil of David, Gros glorified in his paintings the campaigns of Napoléon from the Pyramides to Prussian Eylau.

17 GÉRICAULT, THÉODORE, 1791–1824. "MAMELUCK, DÉFENDANT UN TROMPETTE BLESSÉ", 1818. L.D. 9. ONLY STATE. Very rare. 13½ × 11 in. Original lithograph. Author's Coll.

Géricault's lithographic work consists of seventy-seven pieces executed by himself. Those done before 1822 are his best. The horse plays an important part as theme in nearly all his work as an artist, and he was a great horseman himself. He died from an illness caused by an accident with his horse. He is by far the most important artist who occupied himself seriously with lithography before 1820. His early large stones, including the "English Set", are rare and much sought after—now at high prices ranging from £40 to £100. Some of his best-known paintings are "Radeau de la Meduse", "Officier de chasseur à cheval", "Epsom Derby", etc. His graphic work is catalogued by L. Delteil.

18 GÉRICAULT, THÉODORE. "HORSES EXERCISING", 1821. L.D. 35/III, RARE. Original lithograph. Author's Coll., from the "English Set" printed by Hullmandel. 11¼ × 16 in.

19 GÉRICAULT, THÉODORE. "THE FLEMISH FARRIER", 1821. L.D. 33. ONLY STATE. Original lithograph. Author's Coll., 8⅞ × 12¾ in., from the "English Set" printed by Hullmandel. This set was executed during Géricault's stay in England, 1820–1.

19a GÉRICAULT, THÉODORE. "LION DEVO-RANT UN CHEVAL", 1820. L.D. 26, RARE. Author's Coll., 7¾ × 11⅞ in. Original lithograph executed during his stay in London on a specially prepared cardboard with the pen, an invention of Senefelder as substitute for stone, called in France "Papyrographie" (see text, Part A).

20 CHARLET, NICOLAS-TOUSSAINT, 1792–1845. "LE SOLDAT FRANÇAIS", 1818, LA COMBE 74. Original lithograph. 18 × 13¼ in., published by Delpech. Author's Coll.

Charlet, friend of Géricault, executed about 1,000 lithographs of soldiers, Napoléon and his legend, and some which are humorous in treatment.

21 PRUD'HON, PIERRE PAUL, 1758–1823. "UNE LECTURE", 1822, BERALDI 2, IMPRESSION MOTTE. 7¼ × 5¾ in. Author's Coll.

"Une Lecture" is one of the three original lithographs Prud'hon did towards the end of his life. His etching "Phrosine et Mélidore", Œuvres de Gentil-Bernard, is famous. Paintings: "L'Enlèvement de Psyche", "La Justice et la Vengeance poursuivant le Crime".

22 ORLOWSKI, ALEXANDER, 1777–1832. "SLEDGE RIDE IN RUSSIA", SIGNED AND DATED 1820 before all letters. 22 × 17½ in. Author's Coll.

Of Polish nationality by birth, Orlowski settled in 1801 in St Petersburg. He painted scenes from Polish and Russian daily life in town and country, having some inclination to romanticism: Soldiers, Cossacks, Oriental Horsemen; his lithos covering the same field. His first lithograph, published in 1816, was "Three Horsemen".

23 ORLOWSKI, ALEXANDER (see No. 22). "CAUCASIANS", 1819, before all letters, 17½ × 13½ in. Author's Coll.

23a PROUT, SAMUEL, 1783-1852. "A TRANSFER LITHOGRAPH 1818". Original lithograph from Senefelder's book Course of Lithography, London 1819. 6½ × 8⅞ in. Author's Coll.

This lithograph was published in Senefelder's book as an example of the transfer method he had then already improved. Prout was a water-colourist, who later specialised in architectural drawings. As lithographer he contributed to Baron Taylor's work; like Bonington, he also lithographed for Britannia Delineata, Sketches in Flanders and Germany and other publications on France, Italy and the Rhine, and issued some drawing-books (see text, Part A).

24 WARD, JAMES, 1769–1859. "ADONIS", 1824, ARTIST'S PROOF SIGNED IN PENCIL, 13¼ × 17¾ in. Grundy 17. Author's Coll.

From "Celebrated Horses", a series of fourteen original lithographs by J. Ward.

Ward, an important painter of the romantic school, did eighteen original lithographs altogether. His famous painting "Gordale Scar" is in the Tate Gallery, London. Other paintings, like "Horses Fighting", "Bulls Fighting", "Landscape with Cattle", etc., are in London and provincial museums. He was a brother-in-law of George Morland. His graphic work is catalogued by C. R. Grundy.

25 HILL, DAVID OCTAVIUS, 1802–70. "LANDSCAPE", 1821, 10×14 in. Original lithograph from "Views in Perthshire", an album of thirty lithographs by D. O. Hill. Perth. No date. Gernsheim Coll.

Hill, a Scottish landscape painter and lithographer, has attained world fame through his photographs, being the first artist who used the camera as a medium of expression in 1843, soon after the invention of Fox Talbot's negative process. Hill's photographic portraits are unsurpassed.

26 BEWICK, THOMAS, 1753–1828. "THE CADGER'S TROT", 1823, FIRST STATE, UNIQUE. Original lithograph, 5¾×7 in. Author's Coll.

This first state, hitherto unknown to exist, is reproduced for the first time. It shows that Bewick must have spent some time with the printer, and some trial proofs must have been taken before the twenty prints mentioned by Bell were printed. Bewick did only this one attempt to lithograph; his fame rests as renovator of the woodcut.

27 BEWICK, THOMAS (see No. 26). "THE CADGER'S TROT", 1823, SECOND STATE. Original lithograph. Author's Coll.

This second state differs from the prints in the British Museum and the Victoria & Albert Museum, which are a third state, as in this third state the whole of the horse's hindquarters is covered with an equal tone, so that the lines of the muscles show less, the lower part of the horseman's coat is slightly shaded by about ten more lines behind the upper part of the thigh, the outline of the hoof of the left hind leg is more softened, as well as the right front leg, and a line is added to the landscape top right.

Bewick's graphic work has been catalogued by D. Croal Thomson, but no different states are mentioned there of his only lithograph.

28 BONINGTON, RICHARD PARKES, 1801–28. "RUE DU GROS HORLOGE, ROUEN", 1824, CURTIS 16/II. 9⅝×10 in. First original lithograph of Bonington for Baron Taylor's *Voyages Pittoresques*. Author's Coll.

Bonington, born near Nottingham, studied in Paris, partly under Baron Gros. At the age of twenty-one he received a medal for a water-colour study at the "Salon" in Paris, at the same time as Constable. Friend of Delacroix, he accompanied him to England and worked in Delacroix's studio after his return to Paris. Bonington was a painter of landscapes as well of historical and genre pictures. Besides his paintings in the National Gallery, the best collection of

his work is in the Wallace Collection, London. His lithographs and his one etching are catalogued by Curtis.

28a OTIS, BASS, 1784–1861. EARLY AMERICAN LITHOGRAPH.

Otis, portrait painter, engraver and lithographer. American by birth (New England), worked in New York and Philadelphia. The lithograph reproduced here (see text, Part A) is one of the earliest American specimens.

29 GOYA, FRANCISCO, 1746–1828. LES TAUREAUX DE BORDEAUX, Pl. 4.–1825. "LA DIVISION DE PLACE", L.D. 289, I STATE, 12⅛×16¼ in. Original lithograph. British Museum, Print Coll.

Goya, the great Spanish painter and etcher, started in 1819 to lithograph. His entire lithographic work comprises twenty-three pieces, four of which, the Bullfight scenes, were published by Gaulon in not more than 100 copies. All the other Goya lithographs are excessively rare and exist only in trial-proof state.

Goya's entire graphic work is catalogued by L. Delteil.

30 GOYA, FRANCISCO (see No. 29). "LA DANCE ESPAGNOL", 1825. L.D. 278, ONLY STATE. Original lithograph. 7⅞×7¼ in. Excessively rare. British Museum, Print Coll., executed during his stay in Bordeaux.

31 GOYA, FRANCISCO. LES TAUREAUX DE BORDEAUX, Pl. 3.–1825, "DIVERTISSEMENT D'ESPAGNE", L.D. 288, II STATE, 12⅛×16⅜ in. Original lithograph, 1825. British Museum, Print Coll.

32 GOYA, FRANCISCO. "LE DUEL", DATE DISPUTED. L.D. 278, ONLY STATE. Excessively rare. British Museum, Print Coll.

33 DELACROIX, EUGÈNE, 1798–1863. ILLUSTRATION FOR FAUST, "FAUST ET MEPHISTOPHELES GALOPANT DANS LA NUIT DU SABBAT", 1828. L.D. 73, II STATE OF V. Original lithograph, 8⅛×11¼ in. Author's Coll.

Delacroix, one of the most important figures in French painting of the last century, did a great number of lithographs (about 100). He started in 1817 with some caricatures of no importance for the magazine *Miroir*. His series of "Medailles antiques" (Pl. 34), however, started his career as the greatest lithographer of his time. *Macbeth, Faust, Hamlet, Goetz* and many studies of animals following until 1856. Delacroix, a pupil of Guérin, came under the influence of his friend and colleague Géricault; some of his best-known paintings are: "La Barque du Dante", "Massacres de Scio", "Femmes Algériennes", "Héliodore chassé du temple", "La lutte de Jacob". He also painted battle scenes. In 1832 he travelled to Morocco, which country influenced his art strongly. His graphic work is catalogued by L. Delteil.

34 DELACROIX, EUGÈNE (*see* 33). "FEUILLE DE DOUZE MEDAILLES ANTIQUES", 1825. L.D. 47/III, published by *L'Artiste* in March 1864. Original lithograph, 9¾×12¼ in. Author's Coll.

35 DELACROIX, EUGÈNE. "JEUNE TIGRE JOUANT AVEC SA MERE", 1831. L.D. 91, FIRST STATE OF SIX. 4⅜×7⅜ in. Author's Coll. Original lithograph published by *L'Artiste* in 1831.

36 BARYE, ANTOINE-LOUIS, 1796–1875. "UNE LIONNE ET SES PETITS", 1832. L.D. 3, III/V, 5⅞×9⅛ in. Author's Coll. Original lithograph published by *L'Artiste*.

Barye studied sculpture under Bosio and painting with Gros. He was mainly an animal sculptor, preferring bronze as his medium. He worked also in the Forest of Fontainebleau, where he made studies of landscapes. His lithographs, drawings of animals of a remarkable strength of form and simplification, were mostly published by *L'Artiste*. His graphic work is catalogued by Delteil.

37 DEVERIA, ACHILLE, 1800–1857. "ALEX. DUMAS, PÈRE", 1829. BERALDI 16. 13¼×10 in. Author's Coll.

Deveria, painter and lithographer, pupil of Girodet, did over 400 lithographs, his most famous being his portraits, such as Alex. Dumas, Victor Hugo and Liszt, which outclass his other work.

38 ISABEY, EUGÈNE, 1803–86. "INTERIEUR D'UN PORT", 1833, BERALDI 8, CURTIS 68/I. From the "Second Cahier de Marines", chez Morlot, Paris. 12¼×9¼ in. Author's Coll.

Son of J. B. Isabey, the miniaturist, he painted genre scenes, land- and sea-scapes. His lithographs reveal a great power of expressing colour in a black-and-white design. They are catalogued by Curtis.

39 HUET, PAUL, 1803–69. "COLLINES DE ST SAUVEUR, PRÈS DE ROUEN", 1831, L.D. 59/II. Very rare. 4½×7 in. Author's Coll.

Huet, pupil of Gros, friend of Delacroix and Daumier, was a landscape painter of the romantic school with, however, a lyrical approach to his object. His numerous lithographs are catalogued by Delteil.

40 DUPRÉ, JULES, 1811–89. "PACAGES LIMOUSINS", 1835. L.D. 1/II. Original lithograph. 4½×7¼ in. Published in *L'Artiste*. Author's Coll.

Dupré, friend of Delacroix and Rousseau, painted in the Forest of Fontainebleau. He visited England and came under the influence of Constable. His graphic work is catalogued by Delteil.

41 CHASSÉRIAU, THEODORE, 1819–56. "APOLLON ET DAPHNE", 1844. B. 26, premier tirage. 8⅞×6¼ in. Author's Coll.

Chassériau, pupil of Ingres and disciple of Delacroix, great painter of his time, did only three original lithographs, two of which, "Apollon et Daphne" and "Venus Anadyomène", belong to the *chefs-d'œuvre* of lithography. Both must, however, be seen in early impressions, as the later ones have lost their qualities. He also did twenty-four etchings. His graphic work is catalogued in A. Bouvenne, Théodore Chassériau (*Bulletin des beaux-arts*, 1884) and by Bénédite in 1931.

42 DIAZ DE LA PENA, NARCISSE VIRGIL, 1807–76. "LES FOLLES AMOUREUSES", 1849, published in *L'Artiste*. 7⅝×6½ in. Author's Coll.

Diaz, of Spanish origin, painted in the Forest of Fontainebleau, somewhat influenced by Correggio. The few lithographs he did were published in *L'Artiste*.

43 DAUMIER, HONORÉ, 1808–79. "GUIZOT", 1833, L.D. 74. Published in *La Caricature*. 10½×7⅞ in. Author's Coll.

Daumier, who did about four thousand lithographs, as contributor to *La Caricature* and *Le Charivari*, is today recognised as one of the great painters of his epoch. His entire graphic work is recorded by L. Delteil in ten volumes.

44 DAUMIER, HONORÉ. "LA TETE BRANLANTE", 1834, L.D. 90. Published in *La Caricature*, signed "H.D.". 8⅜×10⅞ in. Author's Coll.

This magnificent design is lesser known than "Le Ventre législative" or "La Rue Transnonain", but easily stands comparison with his best.

45 DAUMIER, HONORE. "CECI A TUE CELA", 1871, L.D. 3845, III/IV. From the *Album de la Siège*, published February 1871. 9⅜×7⅞ in. Author's Coll. An original lithograph related to the Franco-Prussian war and an example of Daumier's last period.

46 GAVARNI, PAUL (C. SULPICE-GUILLAUME CHEVALLIER, DIT), 1804–66. "LE MOSIEU DE LA DEBUTANTE", 1852, BERALDI 248, from the series of twelve original lithographs, "Le Manteau d'Arlequin", published by *L'Eclair*. 7⅞×6½ in. Author's Coll.

Gavarni contributed to almost all illustrated papers of his epoch. He started to lithograph in 1824, producing altogether nearly 2,700 prints. He became Daumier's colleague at the *Charivari* and at one time was in higher esteem than Daumier himself.

47 MENZEL, ADOLF VON, 1815–1905. "BÄRENZWINGER", 1851, Bock 404, from the series "Versuche auf Stein mit Pinsel und Schabeisen" (six original lithographs). 7¾×9¾. British Museum, Print Coll.

Menzel, history painter of greatest importance in Prussia, started as professional lithographer and became one of the most prominent representatives of realism in Germany: *Eisenwalzwerk* (steel-mill). He knew the much younger Courbet, but it would be wrong to say that he was influenced by him. His graphic work is extensive, but though he was an excellent lithographer—with pen and chalk—he sponsored the professional wood-engraver for his illustrative work: *History of Frederick the Great*, *The Writings of Frederick II*, etc. In his later life he was ennobled by the king. His entire graphic work is catalogued by Bock.

48 MANET, ÉDOUARD, 1832–83. "LA BARRICADE", 1871, M.G. 76, PREMIER TIRAGE, AVANT LETTRE, M.N. 82/I. Rare. $18\frac{3}{4}\times13\frac{3}{8}$ in. Author's Coll.

One of two original lithographs depicting the Civil War. Manet, who exercised such a great influence on the development of painting in France, must be regarded as the father of modern lithography, though he did altogether, including those made on transfer-paper, only 24 lithographs. His graphic work is catalogued by Moreau-Nelaton and by Marcel Guérin.

49 MANET, ÉDOUARD. "À LA FENETRE" 1875, M.G. 86, c/II. LITHOGRAPH FOR "THE RAVEN" BY EDGAR POE, TRANSLATED BY STEPHANE MALLARMÉ. $15\frac{1}{8}\times12\frac{1}{4}$. Original lithograph. Author's Coll. Manet illustrated *Le Corbeau* with six lithographs drawn with the brush, using transfer-paper. An edition of 240 copies was printed but remained unsold for the greater part, in spite of the low price (25 Frs. for the ordinary edition and 35 Frs. for the edition with a double set of the four full-page lithographs). Not all copies are signed by the artist and the translator. Complete copies of *The Raven* are very rare, and a copy with a double set must today be valued at about £300, but has not come to light for many years.

50 COROT, CAMILLE, 1796–1875. "SOUVENIR D'ITALIE", 1871. L.D. 27/II. 5×7 in. Author's Coll. One of fifty impressions published in 1872 under the title *Douze croquis et dessins originaux sur papier autographique par Corot*.

"Papier autographique" is transfer-paper as used by many artists, and these "Autographies" are original lithographs, the term used only for technical explanation. Altogether Corot did 18 lithographs. His graphic work is catalogued by Delteil.

51 FANTIN-LATOUR, HENRI, 1836–1904. "SARAH LA BAIGNEUSE", 1892, 3RD PLATE, HEDIARD 99/II, PRESENTATION PROOF. $13\frac{1}{4}\times10\frac{1}{2}$ in. Author's Coll.

Fantin's lithographic work numbers 147 pieces, most of them inspired by Berlioz, Wagner and other musicians. His "Baigneuses" and his "Bouquet de Roses" are his best. He visited England and, as an admirer of Wagner, also Bayreuth. His paintings are groups of portraits of famous contemporaries, an "Hommage à Delacroix" with Whistler, Manet and Baudelaire, and flower-pieces which are highly esteemed today. His graphic work is catalogued by Hédiard.

52 REDON, ODILON, 1840–1916. "TETE DE CHRIST", 1887, MELLERIO 71, one of twenty-five impressions. $13\times10\frac{5}{8}$ in. Author's Coll.

Redon published his first lithographs in 1879, "Dans le Rêve". From 1883–99 he practically abandoned painting for lithography. Some of his famous plates are: "Yeux Clos", "Cheval Ailé", "Pegasus Captive" and his set "Hommage à Goya". He was associated with symbolist writers like Gide, Valèry and Mallarmé. His most important paintings were painted after 1900, oils in fine colour of a dream-like quality, anticipating the surrealist movement. His work is catalogued by Mellerio.

53 REDON, ODILON. "DANS LE DEDALE DES TRANCHES LA BLÈME FIGURE APPARAISSAIT", 1886, MELLERIO 76. $6\frac{1}{8}\times3\frac{7}{8}$ in. Illustration for *Le Juré* by E. Picard, published in a limited edition of 100 copies in 1887. Author's Coll.

54 CARRIÈRE, EUGÈNE, 1849–1906. "MARGUERITE CARRIÈRE", 1901, L.D. 43/II. $17\frac{1}{8}\times13\frac{3}{4}$ in. Author's Coll. Original lithograph printed from two stones.

Carrière, who painted in brownish tones, was connected with the symbolists. The majority of his paintings are portraits, so are his lithographs, the best being his Verlaine, de Goncourt and Marg. Carrière. His graphic work is catalogued by Delteil.

55 GAUGUIN, PAUL 1848–1903. "MANAO TUPAPAU", 1894, M.G. 50. No. 8 of 100 impressions, signed. $7\frac{1}{4}\times10\frac{7}{8}$ in. Coll. Rex Nan Kivell.

This stone was executed by Gauguin in Paris during his stay between his two journeys to Tahiti. It is related to his famous painting of 1892 and published in the second year of *L'Estampe Originale*. Gauguin's woodcuts, in a new and original technique, had great influence on the "Fauves", Munch and the "Expressionists". He also sculptured, made ceramics, and was a writer on art (*Noa-Noa, Avant et Après*, etc.). Gauguin's graphic work is catalogued by Marcel Guérin.

56 GAUGUIN, PAUL. BRETONNES À LA BARRIÈRE, 1889, M.G. 4, one of 50 proofs, printed on yellow paper. $6\frac{3}{4}\times8\frac{5}{8}$ in. Author's Coll. Original lithograph printed from zinc ("dessins au crayon lithographic sur zinc") from a series of eleven prints exhibited at the Café Volpini in 1889. These lithographs are still influenced by his Bretagne period of paintings. They were reprinted later on *simili Japon*.

57 TOULOUSE-LAUTREC, HENRI DE, 1864–1901. "LA GOULUE", 1894, L.D. 71, FIRST STATE, before letters, stamped and numbered. $12\times9\frac{1}{8}$ in. Author's Coll. Designed as cover for a waltz by A. Bosc.

Lautrec's work as lithographer comprises over 350 stones. He did his first lithograph in 1885, an illustration for a song by Bruant, but did not start to lithograph properly until 1891, when he used colour for the first time. His graphic work comprises posters, series of lithographs, like "Elles" and "Yvette Gilbert", single stones as well as illustrations for books (*Histoires Naturelles, Au Pied du Sinai*), book covers, programmes, in colour or black-and-white lithography. The prices paid for his lithographs have enormously increased. A. Arnould, in a catalogue of posters and prints, with a cover by Toulouse-Lautrec, offered in 1896 the colour lithograph "Napoléon" for 20 Frs. in gold (18*s*). The same print, of which 100 impressions were taken, costs today about £400.

58 TOULOUSE-LAUTREC. "LA GOULUE ET SA SŒUR", 1892, L.D. 11. Proof in colour, signed and numbered, stamped by Ancourt. $18 \times 13\frac{3}{4}$ in. Coll. Rex Nan Kivell.

La Goulue and her partner, Valentin le Désossé, at the Moulin Rouge figure in many lithographs and paintings by Lautrec. This lithograph was offered by Arnould in his catalogue (edition 100) in 1896 for 20 Frs. (18*s*), today this plate is not to be found for £400.

59 TOULOUSE-LAUTREC. "MLLE MARCEL LENDER EN BUSTE", 1895, L.D. 102/III. $12\frac{3}{4} \times 9\frac{1}{2}$ in. Author's Coll. Original lithography in eight colours, printed by Ancourt for the German art magazine *Pan* (Vol. I). This lithograph was published in about 1,000 copies, the yearly subscription price for the magazine was then about £1 for four issues. Today this much sought after lithograph costs about £75.

60 DEGAS, EDGAR (DE GAS DIT), 1834–1917. "APRES LE BAIN", *c.* 1885, L.D. 60/IV, FIRST PLATE. $7\frac{1}{2} \times 5\frac{3}{4}$ in. British Museum, Print Coll.

Degas never published his etchings or lithographs, and few impressions therefore exist. Of the group which at one time exhibited together under the name of Impressionists, Degas was the most important engraver and lithographer. He himself regarded this activity more as an experimental one, and he tried all kinds of technical possibilities, which accounts for the many various states which exist of his etchings and lithographs.

61 CÉZANNE, PAUL, 1839–1906. "PORTRAIT DE CÉZANNE", 1898, VENTURI 1158, JOHNSON 31, one of 100 proofs on papier Ingres d'Arches. $12\frac{3}{4} \times 11$ in. Author's Coll.

This lithograph was executed by Cézanne for the third but unpublished album "des peintres-graveurs" by Vollard. Cézanne was not really interested in graphic art, but as a painter he exercised a dominating influence on the development of modern art.

62 SIGNAC, PAUL. "PORT DE ST TROPEZ", 1898, JOHNSON 188. 17×13 in. Original lithograph in four colours. Executed for the third but unpublished *Album des Peintres-Graveurs.*

Signac, who obtained advice first from Monet and Guillaumin, became friend of Seurat and adopted his technique of dividing the colours of the spectrum. He applied the same method in his colour-lithographs, which are less than ten in number. Saint Tropez, the colourful harbour in the South of France he first visited during one of his many sailing trips, became one of his residences. His colour lithographs have become very rare.

63 PISSARRO, CAMILLE, 1830–1903. "BAIGNEUSES À L'OMBRE DES BERGES BOISÉES, 1895, L.D. 142, FIRST STATE, one of 14 proofs. $5\frac{7}{8} \times 8\frac{1}{2}$ in. Author's Coll. Numbered and described by the artist.

Pissarro was the only Impressionist whose graphic work is extensive. The number of his etchings goes beyond the hundred mark, and his lithographs over sixty, ten of which were completed in 1874. In his later work, in the 'nineties, he often used the more convenient zinc plate as substitute for the stone, like Gauguin. The early states of his lithographs are all printed in very small numbers only, and recently much sought after. His graphic work is catalogued by L. Delteil.

64 SISLEY, ALFRED, 1839–1899. "BORD DU LOING, PRÈS DE SAINT MAMMES", 1896, L.D. 5. $5\frac{1}{2} \times 8\frac{5}{8}$ in., printed in sepia. Author's Coll. Sisley's only original lithograph. (L.D. 6 in colour was done with the assistance of the printer Clot.)

Sisley, landscape painter in the technique of the Impressionists, though born in Paris was of British nationality, and remained so until his death. This one example of lithography he did is the best landscape lithograph drawn in black-and-white in the style and technique of the Impressionists. His graphic work is catalogued by L. Delteil.

65 RENOIR, AUGUSTE, 1841–1919. "ODALISQUE", 1904, L.D. 35, R.-M. 10. $3\frac{1}{8} \times 4\frac{3}{4}$ in. Author's Coll.

This original lithograph was drawn on stone as a frontispiece for a book, which was never published. Seventy-five impressions were taken.

Renoir, a painter of great eminence, is not of the same importance as a graphic artist, though he did a fair number of etchings and lithographs, in which he repeated himself quite frequently. His colour lithographs were executed with the assistance of the printer Clot, losing therefore the claim to be regarded as original lithographs.

66 RENOIR, AUGUSTE. "RICHARD WAGNER", *c.* 1900, L.D. 33, R.-M.8. $16\frac{5}{8} \times 12\frac{5}{8}$ in. This impression signed in pencil by the artist. Author's Coll. Rare.

Renoir visited Wagner in Palermo during the winter of 1881–2 and painted a portrait of him, which served later for this original lithograph. Other portrait-lithographs are his Cézanne, Rodin, Vollard and Mlle Dieterle. His graphic work is catalogued by Delteil and Roger-Marx.

67 BONNARD, PIERRE, 1867–1947. "GARDE MUNICIPAL", 1893, TERR. 7, R.-M. 26. $9\frac{3}{8} \times 5\frac{7}{8}$ in. Author's Coll., signed and numbered. Published in *L'Escarmouche*.

Bonnard, original member of the "Nabis", had a decisive influence on the revival of lithography in the 'nineties. He even preceded Lautrec with his poster "France-Champagne" in 1889. His lithographs in colour and black-and-white were published by *La Revue Blanche*, *L'Escarmouche*, *L'Estampe et L'Affiche*, and the *Insel*. His set of 12 colour lithographs "Quelques Aspects de la Vie de Paris" was published by Vollard. He illustrated books in the same technique, and continued to lithograph until his last years. His work as a lithographer is just as much sought after as the one of Lautrec, and today £50 to £120 is paid for his colour plates. His graphic work is catalogued by Terrasse and Roger-Marx.

68 BONNARD, PIERRE. "LES BOULE-VARDS", 1899, TERR. 41, R.-M. 74. Original litho-graph in colour. $10\frac{1}{4} \times 13\frac{7}{8}$ in. Author's Coll. Published by the German *Insel* in an edition of 100 copies in 1900. One of the finest colour lithographs by Bonnard.

69 BONNARD, PIERRE. "FEMME ASSISE DANS SA BAIGNOIRE", 1942, R.-M. 78. Original lithograph printed in nine tones. $11\frac{1}{2} \times 9\frac{5}{8}$ in. Author's Coll. One of Bonnard's last lithographs corresponding to the style of painting he had developed at Le Cannet in the South of France, where he spent the last six years of his life.

70 VUILLARD, ÉDOUARD, 1868–1940. "JEUNE FEMME ACCOUDÉE", 1894, R.-M. 26, VERY RARE. Signed. $6\frac{7}{8} \times 4\frac{7}{8}$ in. Author's Coll.

Next to Bonnard, his friend and colleague with the "Nabis", Vuillard is the most important graphic artist around the turn of the century. His graphic work is catalogued by Roger-Marx.

71 VUILLARD, EDOUARD. "INTERIEUR A LA SUSPENSION", 1899, R.-M. 35/III, JOHNSON 200, 5. From the album *Paysages et Intérieurs*, published by Vollard. $4\frac{1}{4} \times 11$ in. Coll. Rex Nan Kivell. Original lithograph in five colours.

72 DENIS, MAURICE, 1870–1943. "MÈRE ET ENFANT", 1897. Published in *Pan*. $9\frac{5}{8} \times 6\frac{3}{4}$. Author's Coll. Printed in grey.

Denis, spokesman of the "Nabis", moved later towards a "Neo-Classicism" in his paintings, which also expresses itself in his lithographs in colour and black-and-white.

73 WHISTLER, JAMES ABBOTT McNEILL, 1834–1903. "EARLY MORNING", 1879, WAY 7/II. Original lithotint. $6\frac{1}{2} \times 10\frac{1}{4}$ in. British Museum, Print Room Coll.

Whistler held, and still occupies, an important position in the history of etching. His lithographic work, with the exception of his lithotints and a few drawings of nudes, is, however, not very convincing. "Early Morning" (reproduced here) clearly shows Japanese influence.

American-born Whistler, though he had his permanent residence in England, was just as much at home in France. He was made an Officer of the Legion of Honour and was President of the Society of British Artists. Of his oils, the best known are "Portrait of his Mother", "Carlyle," and his "River Scenes at Dusk". His lithographs are cata-logued by Way.

74 WHISTLER, JAMES McNEILL. "NUDE MODEL, RECLINING", 1893, WAY 47. $4\frac{1}{2} \times 8\frac{3}{8}$ in. British Museum, Print Room Coll.

75 STEER, PHILIP WILSON, O.M., 1860–1942. "THE NURSEMAID", 1892. Original lithograph pub-lished in *Albemarle*. $5\frac{1}{2} \times 8\frac{1}{4}$ in. Author's Coll.

Steer, representative of Impressionism in England, but strongly influenced by Constable and Gainsborough in his paintings, did only a few lithographs.

76 SICKERT, WALTER RICHARD, 1860–1942. "CAT'S CRADLE", 1892. Original lithograph published in *Albemarle*. $6\frac{1}{2} \times 9$ in. Author's Coll.

Sickert, born at Munich, pupil of Whistler, friend of Degas, was the 'premier' representative of Impressionistic technique in England, which he underlined with a strong pictorial outlook. In 1911 he founded the Camden Town Group. The number of his etchings is considerable, but he did very few lithographs. He was an accomplished writer on art, with strong views. An article he had written in the *Saturday Review* resulted in an action by Pennell in the High Court, which Sickert lost, as his article lacked foundation.

77 SICKERT, WALTER RICHARD. "WOMAN WITH HAT", 1907. Original lithograph for *Neolith*. $13 \times 8\frac{1}{2}$ in. Signed first proof. Author's Coll. An excellent drawing somewhat influenced by Degas.

78 JOHN, AUGUSTUS, O.M., R.A., BORN 1878. "THE BATHERS", 1921, D.3. Published by the Leicester Galleries for the Senefelder Club. $12 \times 14\frac{3}{4}$ in. Author's Coll.

John, best known here and in America for his portraits, is an individualist of great gifts, on whom the modern movement in art left no impression. His drawings of heads and figures are highly estimated. His etchings are numerous and catalogued by Dodgson. His lithographs are few, but representative of John as draughtsman.

79 THOMA, HANS, 1839–1924. "PORTRAIT OF HANS THOMA", 1894, BERINGER 51. Original lithograph from three stones. $18 \times 14\frac{1}{2}$ in. Author's Coll. Presentation proof.

Pupil of Schirmer, influenced by Courbet, Thoma painted landscapes, biblical scenes and allegories of strong effects. In his old age he became, however, too literary, his best work being before 1914. He took great interest in the graphic arts, and was one of the first painters in Germany to revive lithography, which he started to practise in 1892. By using colour at this early stage he influenced the development of lithography in Germany. His graphic work is catalogued by Beringer.

80 LIEBERMANN, MAX, 1847–1935. ILLUS-TRATION ZU KLEISTS KLEINE SCHRIFTEN. "REITER KAMPF", 1917. Schiefler 233. $4 \times 6\frac{1}{2}$ in. Author's Coll.

Liebermann, first influenced by Millet and the School of Barbizon, later by French Impressionism and Degas (he himself collected paintings by Manet, Degas and Cézanne), did not start to lithograph until 1896. In later years he illustrated books in this medium. His graphic work is catalogued by Schiefler.

81 SLEVOGT, MAX, 1868–1932. "DIE INSELN WAK WAK", 1921. Original lithographs by Slevogt. Ruemann 49. Victoria & Albert Museum Coll.

The importance of the painter Slevogt rests with his lithographic illustrations, which caused a renaissance of the finely printed and illustrated book in Germany.

82 CORINTH, LOVIS, 1858–1925. "DIE ERSCHAFFUNG ADAMS", 1923. Original lithograph in colour from the set "Im Paradies", trial proof on Japon. $14 \times 12\frac{1}{2}$ in. Author's Coll. Subsequent to Schwarz.

Born in East Prussia, the son of a tanner, Corinth spent much of his time in the slaughter-house, witnessing scenes which influenced him later in his paintings. His large figure paintings are bold with a vivid texture and somewhat baroque. His extensive graphic work is catalogued by Schwartz. Corinth was, without doubt, the greatest German painter around the turn of the century.

83 KOLLWITZ, KÄTHE, 1867–1945. "POR-TRAIT OF THE ARTIST", 1920, WAGNER 137. $9\frac{1}{4} \times 8$ in. Author's Coll.

In the life of Käthe Kollwitz as an artist the graphic arts occupy the first place. Though she did a number of litho-graphs, her etched work is preponderant. Her work is catalogued by Sievers and by Wagner.

84 MUNCH, EDVARD, 1863–1944. "GESCHREI" 1895, Schiefler 32. $13\frac{3}{4} \times 9\frac{7}{8}$ in. Original lithograph. An example of Munch's early period.

The Norwegian Edvard Munch, a solitary figure in Scandinavian painting, contemporary of Ibsen, paved the way for Expressionism in Germany, the country where his genius was first acknowledged. His graphic work,

catalogued by Schiefler up till 1926, comprises about 500 numbers.

84a MUNCH, EDVARD. "TINGEL-TANGEL", 1895, Schiefler 37. Original lithograph. $16\frac{1}{8} \times 24\frac{3}{4}$ in. Mun. Museum, Oslo (*see* text, Part A).

85 MUNCH, EDVARD. "FRAUENBILDNIS MIT SCHWARZEM SCHAL", 1920, Sch.476. Origi-nal Lithograph. Proof with the notes in Munch's hand-writing, "Drucke" and "Stein vernichten". $18\frac{1}{2} \times 14$ in. Author's Coll. An example of Munch's later period.

86 KOKOSCHKA, OSKAR, BORN 1886 IN PÖCHLARN (AUSTRIA), LIVES IN LONDON AND SWITZERLAND. "DER FUCHS UND DIE TRAU-BEN", 1952. Original lithograph in colour. Artist's proof. $16\frac{1}{4} \times 22\frac{1}{8}$ in. Author's Coll. Published by "Guilde de la Gravure", Genève.

Kokoschka, an important figure in Central European art between the two wars, has expressed himself frequently through the medium of lithography, and used it for illus-trating his own writings (*Der gefesselte Kolumbus*, 1913, *Hiob*, 1918), and *Karl Kraus: Die Chinesische Mauer*, 1914 and the portfolio of *Bachkantate*, 1915. He also lithographed many portraits and single stones. The graphic catalogue by Arntz will be brought up to date by a new catalogue of his work by Hans Maria Wingler. Kokoschka was Professor of painting in Dresden and, after the Anschluss, Professor in Prague. Since 1938 he has lived in London, making frequent trips to the U.S.A., where his paintings are to be found in most public galleries of importance. He also lives at a house he built near Lake Geneva.

87 KOKOSCHKA, OSKAR. "ILLUSTRATION ZU HIOB", 1918. $11\frac{1}{2} \times 9\frac{1}{2}$ in. Ein Drama mit 14 Orig. Lithographien bei O. Kokoschka, Berlin 1918, Casirer. One of 100 copies. Author's Coll.

88 NOLDE, EMIL, BORN 1867 IN NOLDE, GERMANY. "FABELTIERE", 1926. Original litho-graph in colour. $6\frac{1}{2} \times 4\frac{3}{4}$ in. Published in the limited edition of *Nolde*, Vol. II, by Schiefler. Author's Coll.

Nolde, at one time associated with the *Brücke*, is the foremost figure of the German Expressionists, without sharing their shortcomings. During the Hitler regime Nolde was "Malverbot" (he was forbidden to paint) from 1941 onwards. He holds the title of Professor and Doctor H.C., and received the prize for graphic art at the Venice Biennale, 1952. His graphic work comprises well over 400 pieces, and is catalogued by Schiefler in two volumes.

89 KANDINSKY, WASSILY, 1866–1944. "KOM-POSITION MIT BLAUEM KEIL", 1922. Original litho-graph printed in five colours on Japon, signed. $10\frac{1}{2} \times 9\frac{1}{2}$ in. Author's Coll.

Russian-born Kandinsky studied in Munich in 1896

After extensive travels and a short stay in Paris, he settled in Munich in 1908. It was there that he painted his first abstract works (water-colours and drawings). In 1922 he became Professor at the "Bauhaus" in Weimar and Dessau, and finally in Berlin. He left Germany in 1933 for France (Neuilly-sur-Seine), where he died in 1944. He wrote two important books on art: in 1910 *Uber das Geistige in der Kunst*, published in 1912, and *Punkt und Linie zu Fläche*, published 1926. In 1911 he founded, together with Marc and Macke, the "Blaue Reiter" movement.

Greatly interested in graphic art, he illustrated his poems *Klänge* with colour woodcuts (1913) and published an album, *Kleine Welten* (woodcuts, etchings and lithographs in colour). His graphic work contains also a number of single lithographs in colour, closely related to his abstract paintings. A catalogue of his graphic work by W. Grohmann is in preparation.

90 KIRCHNER, ERNST LUDWIG, 1880–1938. "PORTRAIT CARL STERHEIM", 1916. 12½×8¼ in. Published in the *Bildermann* by Cassirer, Berlin. Author's Coll.

Kirchner, who originally studied architecture, became a founder member of *Die Brücke*. In 1916 he settled in Davos (Switzerland), where he remained until his death. His extensive graphic work (about 1,500 numbers) is catalogued by Schiefler in two volumes.

91 KLEE, PAUL, 1879–1940. "DIE HEXE MIT DEM KAMM", 1922/107, Soby 29. Original lithograph. 12×8⅝ in., signed. Author's Coll.

Klee studied in Munich under Knirr and Franz v. Stuck (1898–1902), and settled there in 1906. First under the influence of Kubin, he became associated with Kandinsky and the "Blaue Reiter". German by birth, he was called up during the First World War from 1916–18. In 1921 he was appointed Professor at the "Bauhaus" in Weimar and Dessau, in 1930 Professor at the Academy of Düsseldorf. He was deprived of his position by the Nazis, his works were banned, and he went to Switzerland at the end of 1933. The making of prints was suitable for Klee and his art, his entire graphic work comprises over 150 prints, catalogued by J. T. Soby.

92 KLEE, PAUL. "IM GEISTE HOFFMANNS", 1921/123, Soby 26. Original lithograph in four colours. 12½×9 in., signed. Coll. Rex Nan Kivell.

93 BECKMANN, MAX, 1884–1950. "PIERROT UND MASKE", 1920, GLASER 152. Original lithograph. 12¼×8 in. Author's Coll.

Beckmann, originally influenced by the Impressionists, did not develop his own style until 1917, after having experienced the movement of "Die Brücke". From 1925–33 he was Professor in Frankfurt, in 1937 he left Germany for Holland, where he lived in Amsterdam until 1947, when he emigrated to the U.S.A. His graphic work is considerable, and catalogued, up till 1923, by C. Glaser in the "Beckmann-Work".

94 MATISSE, HENRI, BORN 1869, LIVES AT NICE, A.M. "DANSEUSE COUCHÉE", ABOUT 1928. 10¾×17¾ in. Signed and numbered. Author's Coll. From the series of ten lithographs "Danseuses".

After having completed his studies at the Academy Julian and with Gustave Moreau in Paris, Matisse did not discover his own ground until 1904, at the age of thirty-four, when he painted some landscapes in flat colours at St Tropez and Pont St Michel. In his picture "Le Tapis Rouge", painted in 1906, the Matisse we know today already reveals himself. Since 1916 Matisse resides at the Côte d'Azur. One of his latest creations is "La Chapelle des sœurs des Dominicaines" at Vence, for which he designed the entire interior decoration in black-and-white, adding colour through the stained-glass windows and the vestments of the priests. His graphic work is considerable, his lithographs dominating. They show him as the outstanding draughtsman he is. He also illustrated and designed a great number of books in all three graphic mediums. A catalogue of his graphic work has been assembled by Duthuit, but remains unpublished.

95 MATISSE, HENRI. "NUE À LA COUPE DE FRUITS", 1926, DUTHUIT 84. 17×21¼ in. No. 5/50. Victoria & Albert Museum, Print Coll.

96 MATISSE, HENRI. "PERSANE", 1929, D. 100. 17½×11¼ in. Victoria & Albert Museum, Print Coll.

97 VLAMINCK, MAURICE DE, BORN 1876 IN PARIS OF A BELGIAN FATHER. "LE PONT DE CHATOU", ABOUT 1927. 9⅝×13¼ in. Original lithograph in colour, signed and stamped. Author's Coll. Published by Frapier (Galerie des Peintres-Graveurs).

Vlaminck, one of the original "Fauves", developed into a landscape painter of poetic-dramatic outlook, preferring sombre colours interwoven with some bright patches. His graphic work is considerable. He illustrated a good number of books with lithographs and woodcuts.

98 UTRILLO, MAURICE, BORN 1883, LIVES IN FRANCE. "MONTMARTRE", 1944. 10×9 in. Original lithograph published as frontispiece to *Utrillo* by Maximilien Gautier, Edit. du Chêne, Paris, 1944. Author's Coll.

Utrillo, son of Suzanne Valadon, the woman painter, is well known and admired for his paintings of street scenes in Paris and the Suburbs and of country towns. These pictures are usually landscapes with architecture in his own inimitable style.

99 DERAIN, ANDRÉ, BORN 1880, LIVES IN FRANCE. "VISAGE", ABOUT 1925. 11½×14 in., signed and numbered, original lithograph from the series "Visages". Author's Coll.

Derain, friend of Matisse and Vlaminck, one of the original "Fauves", with inclinations to Classicism, absorbed the influence of Cézanne and Cubism to arrive at some style of his own. He illustrated a great number of books in all three graphic mediums, his most important being *Rabelais, Pantagruel*, using colour woodcuts, published by Skira in 1946.

100 CHAGALL, MARC, BORN 1887, IN RUSSIA, LIVES AT VENCE A.M. "LE PEINTRE ET SON MODELE", 1952. $16\frac{3}{4} \times 12\frac{1}{2}$ in. Artist's proof. Author's Coll. Edition published by Galerie Maeght.

Russian-born Chagall, an international figure (first one-man show in Berlin in 1914 at *Der Sturm*, Ballet Designer and Commissar for Fine Arts at Vitebsk 1918, returned to Paris 1922, emigrated to New York 1941, returned to France 1948), is an artist of great originality and master in the use of colour, having followers in all countries of the world. His graphic work is very considerable, his illustrations for the Bible (etchings) and many other books are of the highest quality. His colour lithographs for *Arabian Nights* are unique in artistic conception and technical perfectness. He received the prize for graphic art at the Venice Biennale 1950.

101 CHAGALL, MARC. "VISION DE PARIS", 1952. $13\frac{7}{8} \times 10\frac{1}{2}$ in. Original lithograph in colour. Author's Coll. Published by Tériade in *Verve*, the left-hand one of two designs on one stone.

102 DUFY, RAOUL, 1877–1953. "GRANDE BAIGNEUSE", ABOUT 1927. $20\frac{1}{4} \times 26\frac{1}{4}$ in. Original lithograph in colour. Coll. Rex Nan Kivell.

Influenced by Matisse, associate of the "Fauves", Dufy developed his own original style of painting, colour always playing a predominant part. As graphic artist Dufy's importance rests in the first line with his woodcuts. He not only used them for illustrative purposes (Guillaume Apollinaire's *Le Bestiaire*) but also in connection with Paul Poiret, the fashion designer, for textile printing. In later years he aimed at reducing the number of colours he used to a minimum. He illustrated a great many books in various mediums.

103 GRIS, JUAN, 1887–1927. "LA CARTE LETTRE" 1921. $10\frac{1}{4} \times 8\frac{3}{4}$ in. Trial proof on "chine". Author's Coll. Original lithographic illustration to Max Jacob's *Ne coupez pas Mademoiselle*, published by Galerie Simon, Paris 1921 (Kahnweiler).

Gris, actual name José Victoriano Gonzales, Spaniard by birth, came to Paris in 1906, where he met Picasso and the "Poets". He first made drawings for various Paris papers and started to paint in 1910. Gris became one of the cornerstones of Cubist painting, which he developed in his own way. His work is of a clear architectural construction, the objects he depicts often being developed from this construction into forms. He did only a few lithographs, some of which were illustrations for books, all published by the Galerie Simon, where D. H. Kahnweiler backed him until his premature death.

104 BRAQUE, GEORGES, BORN 1882, LIVES IN PARIS AND VARENGEVILLE. "NATURE MORTE", 1921. $8 \times 15\frac{1}{2}$ in. Dedication proof. Author's Coll. Original lithograph in colour. Published 1921 by Galerie Simon in an edition of 120 copies.

Braque, one of the originators of Cubism, is foremost a painter, probably the most important French living painter. His themes are primarily still-lifes, some landscapes, and a very few figure paintings. His graphic work is not extensive, his lithographs in colour belong to his best. (A clear distinction has to be made, however, between Braque's original lithographs, that means between those he did himself and between lithographs reproducing his paintings and drawings done by a professional lithographer or reproduced mechanically in lithographic technique. These last are only reproductions and lack completely Braque's great sense for the graphic arts.)

105 BRAQUE, GEORGES. "THEIÈRE ET CITRON", 1947. $14\frac{1}{4} \times 21\frac{1}{2}$ in. Original lithograph signed and numbered. Coll. Rex Nan Kivell. Published by Galerie Maeght.

106 PICASSO, PABLO, BORN 1881, LIVES AT VALLAURIS AND PARIS. "LA COIFFURE", 1923, MOURLOT 14. $6\frac{1}{2} \times 10\frac{1}{4}$ in. ONLY STATE. One of 50 impressions. Signed and numbered. Author's Coll. Published by Galerie Simon.

Picasso, Spanish-born in Andalusia, painter, sculptor, potter, graphic artist and draughtsman, is the phenomenon of our time. Already in 1910 the painter W. Kandinsky wrote: "Picasso, always guided by an inner force to express himself, often carried away impetuously, throws himself from one medium of expression to the other. If there is an abyss in between, Picasso takes a wild jump—and there he stands on the other side, shocking the enormous number of his followers."

Of all living artists Picasso's lithographic works are the largest in number. Between 1947 and 1949 he has devoted most of his time to lithography, exploring all possible technical means, inventing some new processes used mainly in his lithographs of animals. The stone reproduced here belongs to one of Picasso's earliest lithographs and corresponds with his style of painting at that time. His lithographs are catalogued by Mourlot in two volumes.

107 PICASSO, PABLO. "SCENE D'INTÉRIEUR", 1926, MOURLOT 21. $11\frac{1}{4} \times 8\frac{3}{4}$ in. ONLY STATE. Printer's proof. Author's Coll. Published by Galerie Simon in 100 copies.

108 PICASSO, PABLO. "LE PEINTRE ET SON MODELE", 1930, MOURLOT 27. $9\frac{1}{8} \times 11\frac{1}{2}$ in. ONLY

STATE. Printer's proof. Author's Coll. Published in 50 copies by *Chronique du Jour*. The last lithograph Picasso did before resuming this art in 1945.

109 PICASSO, PABLO. "FIGURE AU CORSAGE RAYÉ", 1949, MOURLOT 179. 25⅞×19⅝ in. Original lithograph in six colours transferred to the stone. One of five trial proofs, lent by Galerie Louise Leiris. Hitherto unpublished, only these five proofs were taken. Stone preserved for further work on it.

110 ROUAULT, GEORGES, BORN 1871, LIVES IN PARIS. "BONIMENT DU CLOWN", ABOUT 1929. 13¼×8 in. First state, one of ten impressions, signed and numbered, *timbre sec* of Frapier (Galerie des Peintres-Graveurs). Author's Coll.

Rouault, originally an apprentice in a glass-painter's studio, later a pupil of Gustave Moreau, exhibited at one time together with the "Fauves". But soon his art developed in an entirely different direction, often described as "Expressionism". He is a Roman Catholic, and his many paintings of religious subjects, painted in his own colourful and inimitable style, testify that they are creations of his conviction. As a graphic artist Rouault is best known by his aquatints in colour and his large plates for *Miserere et Guerre* and *Cirque*, which are executed in a mixture of various techniques. With some of these large plates it seems most likely that besides aquatint a photographic process was involved in procuring them, which would make them doubtful as "original" work by the artist. There can be no dispute, however, with regard to his lithographs, most of them executed with the brush in wash direct on to the stone, afterwards reinforced and worked over with the scraper and some limited use of chalk. Most of them are issued by Frapier (Galerie des Peintres-Graveurs) and stamped with a dry-stamp. They were printed in a very limited number only, and the early states especially are excessively rare.

111 ERNST, MAX, BORN 1891 IN GERMANY, LIVES IN PARIS. "COMPOSITION", 1950. 9¼×7 in. Original lithograph in colour, artist's proof signed and numbered. Author's Coll. Published as frontispiece for the "edition de luxe" of the catalogue of the Ernst Exhibition, 1950, at the Galerie Drouin, Paris (edition of 50 copies).

Though Marc Chagall opened the way for modern surrealist painting in 1911, he continued on a different route, and Max Ernst must be regarded as the foremost exponent of modern surrealism (others are Dali and Tanguy). Ernst, discoverer of "collage" and "frottage", also illustrated books.

112 MASSON, ANDRÉ, BORN 1896, LIVES AT AIX-EN-PROVENCE. "MATERNITÉ", 1951. Original lithograph printed in dark green. 14½×12⅜ in. One of 20 copies. Published by Galerie Louise Leiris, Paris. Author's Coll.

Original member of the Surrealist Movement, Masson strode far beyond its limits, always seeking new ways of expression and further development of his art, sometimes even using Impressionistic formulas. Internationally well known as painter and graphic artist, Masson lived in the U.S.A. from 1942-5. He illustrated a great number of books with etchings and lithographs. His lithographs always reflect the style of his paintings during various periods.

113 MARINI, MARINO, BORN 1901, LIVES AT MILAN. "CHEVAUX", 1951. 18¾×12⅝ in. Original lithograph in three colours, published by "Guilde Internationale de la Gravure", Genève–Paris. Coll. Rex Nan Kivell.

Marini, best known for his sculptures executed in bronze or carved in wood, has also occupied himself a great deal with the graphic arts.

114 CHIRICO, GIORGIO DE, BORN 1888 IN GREECE, OF ITALIAN PARENTS. "GLADIATORS", ABOUT 1929. Original lithograph in colour. 12⅛×16⅜ in. From the series of six lithographs "Metamorphosis". Author's Coll.

Chirico presented his dream world within a strong architectural and geometrical construction, using strange perspective, often opposed to each other, thus creating paintings of a deep inner meaning. In 1934, when, apparently, he had arrived at a cul-de-sac, he denounced his previous work in order to take up painting in "academic" style. He has illustrated books, mainly in lithography.

115 CAMPIGLI, MASSIMO, BORN 1895, LIVES AT ROME. "LE COLLIER", 1952. 13×19¼ in. Original lithograph in three colours, published by "Guilde Internationale de la Gravure", Genève–Paris. Author's Coll.

Campigli started as a journalist but soon changed over to painting. His lithographic work is considerable and identical with the style of his paintings.

116 GIACOMETTI, ALBERTO, BORN 1901 IN SWITZERLAND, LIVES IN PARIS. "L'ATELIER", 1952. 15×11 in. Author's Coll. Original lithograph published in *Derrière le Miroir*, Galerie Maeght, Paris.

Swiss sculptor Giacometti, creator of new forms in space, has only recently started to lithograph. His prints are closely related to his paintings and drawings.

117 LÉGER, FERNAND, BORN 1881, LIVES IN PARIS AND NORMANDY. "COMPOSITION AVEC TÊTE EN PROFIL", 1948. Original lithograph in five colours. 14×19¾ in. Author's Coll. One of 75 copies signed and numbered, published by Galerie Louise Leiris, Paris.

Originally trained as an architect, Léger studied painting in Paris at the "École des Beaux Arts" and others. After a period during which he was under the influence of Impressionism and Divisionism, and later of Cézanne, he arrived at a Cubist technique through discoveries of his own. His love for architecture resulted in his "Sculptures Polychromes" he started to make in 1950. A large example of one of these, done in 1952, is in the "Colombe d'Or" at St Paul, A.M. Though his first lithograph dates from 1920, he did not produce lithographs on a large scale until 1947, and then mainly in colour. He illustrated also a number of books, the most important being *Cirque*, which contained 60 lithographs in colour, published in 1950 by Tériade, the publisher of *Verve* in Paris. Léger is the only great painter of the "old guard" in France who teaches at an art school (Academie Montmartre).

118 MIRO, JOAN, BORN 1893, LIVES IN BARCELONA. "COMPOSITION AVEC DES POUTRES CROISÉES", *c.* 1948. Original lithograph. 9¾×12¾ in. One of 75 copies, signed and numbered. Author's Coll.

Miro, influenced by surrealism, developed his own personal language of forms and signs, colour playing an important part. His art is most suited for lithography as a medium of expression, his graphic work extensive, and mostly published by Galerie Maeght in Paris.

119 NASH, PAUL, 1889–1946. "MINE CRATER, HILL 60", 1917. Original lithograph. 13¾×17⅞ in. One of 25 copies, signed and numbered. Author's Coll.

Nash, painter and great water-colourist, continuing the English tradition, went through the First World War at the Front. His experiences are documented in paintings like "Menin Road" and in a few lithographs and in drawings. He was influenced by Surrealism. He painted his most important oils during and immediately after the Second World War. The woodcuts he did as a book illustrator are the most important contributions he made to the graphic arts. He was probably the foremost artist of his generation in Britain.

120 HODGKINS, FRANCES, 1869–1947. "ARRANGEMENT OF JUGS", 1938. Original lithograph in colour. 18⅜×24½ in. Signed in pencil. Author's Coll. Published by Contemporary Lithographs, London.

The only lithograph by Frances Hodgkins. Born in New Zealand, Miss Hodgkins settled in Paris in 1902, where she gained a certain reputation for her water-colours, which led to her appointment as a teacher at Colarossi's School, one of the best known in Paris. One year later she opened her own school of water-colour painting for women. In 1914 she came to England and

took up oil painting in 1919. But it was not until about 1925, after she had abandoned Impressionism entirely, that she found her own style and way of expression. The last years of her life she spent at Corfe Castle, a village in Dorset, working right up to her death.

121 MOORE, HENRY, BORN 1898, LIVES IN HERTFORDSHIRE. "PROMÉTHÉE", 1950. 13¼×10¼ in. Signed artist's proof. Author's Coll. One of eight original lithographs in colour illustrating Goethe's *Prometheus*, translated by André Gide.

Moore, recognized as the leading British sculptor of today, was born in Yorkshire. He studied at Leeds School of Art and the Royal College in London. His work is to be found in the principal museums of Europe and the U.S.A. As an official war artist during the last war he did a series of shelter drawings of great importance. His shelter sketchbook was published in facsimile by *Poetry London*. His lithographs are few in number, as only in recent years has he taken some interest in this medium.

122 SUTHERLAND, GRAHAM, BORN 1903, LIVES IN KENT. "THREE STANDING FORMS", 1950. Original lithograph transferred from paper to stone. 17½×17⅝ in. Second state, one of three impressions (the stone disintegrated after three impressions had been taken).

Sutherland, the outstanding painter of his generation in Britain, often described as a 'landscapist', started as a graphic artist, preferring etching to any other medium. He did not paint seriously until about 1933, after having abandoned etching entirely. His first lithographs date approximately from the same time, and are in colour. In recent years he has applied himself more frequently to this medium. He has also painted and drawn some portraits and did some tapestry design. At the moment he is engaged with the design for a tapestry for Coventry Cathedral, which will be the world's largest tapestry when completed.

123 SUTHERLAND, GRAHAM. "STUDY, LA PETITE AFRIQUE", 1953. Original lithograph. 22½×17¾ in. Second state, first trial proof. Author's Coll. Drawn on paper and transferred to zinc, on which the artist continued to work.

This lithograph executed by Sutherland in 1953 completes the array of "150 Years of Artists' Lithographs", the first ones being printed and published in England under the name of "Polyautographs", the last one being designed by a British artist and printed in England by the Curwen Press at Plaistow.

BIBLIOGRAPHY

GENERAL

RAPP, H. *Das Geheimnis der Steindruckerey.* Tübingen 1810.

BANKS, H. *Lithography or the art of making drawings on stone.* Bath 1813. Second edition 1816.

SENEFELDER, A. *Vollständiges Lehrbuch der Steindruckerey.* München 1818.
A complete course of Lithography. London 1819.
L'Art de la Lithographie. Munich 1819.
Italian edition. Napoli 1824.

ENGELMANN, G. Rapport sur la lithographie introduite en France par G. E. de Mulhausen (Haut Rhin) 1815.
Manuel du dessinateur lithographe. Paris 1822.
Rapport sur la Chromolithographie. Mulhouse 1837.
Traité théorique et pratique de Lithographie. Mulhouse, s.d. (1838).

HULLMANDEL, C. *The Art of Drawing on Stone.* London 1824.

FERCHL, F. M. *Übersicht der besten und einzigen Incunabel Sammlung der Lithographie.* München 1856.

BOUCHOT, H. *La Lithographie.* Paris 1895.

BÉRALDI, H. *Les Graveurs du XIXe siècle.* 12 vol. Paris 1885–92.

GESELLSCHAFT FÜR VERVIELFÄLTIGENDE KUNST. *Die vervielfältigende Kunst der Gegenwart* Vol. IV Lithographie. Wien 1887–1903.

AUFSEESSER, JUL. "Künstlerische Frühdrucke der Lithographie". *Zeitschrift f. Bücherfreunde, I Jahrg.* Heft III, June 1897.

VELHAGEN U. KLASINGS MONATSHEFTE. "Die Einführung der Steindruckerei in Berlin." 1904/II.

GRÄFF, WALTER. "Die Anfänge der Lithographie in Frankreich". *Ges. für vervielf. Kunst,* Wien 1904.
Die Einführung der Lithographie in Frankreich. Heidelberg 1906.

DUSSLER, L. *Die Inkunabeln der Deutschen Lithographie.* Berlin 1928.
"Ergänzungen zu Dussler". *Münchner Jahrbuch der Bildenden Kunst.* 1929.

MEIER-GRAEFE, JUL. *Entwicklungsgeschichte der modernen Kunst.* 3 vol. München, 1903–04.

PENNELL, JOS. AND E. R. *Lithography and Lithographers.* London 1898 and 1915.

WATT. P. B. "Early English Lithography". *The Artist,* London, May 1896.

PENNELL, JOSEPH. "The truth about Lithography". *The Studio,* London 1899.

SICKERT, WALTER. "The Old Ladies of Etching-needle Street". *The English Review,* London Jan. 1912.

WAGNER, CARL. *Alois Senefelder sein Leben und Wirken.* Leipzig 1914.

SINGER, H. W. *Die Moderne Graphik.* Leipzig 1914.

HARTLAUB, G. *Die neue Deutsche Graphik.* Berlin 1920.
Die Graphik des Expressionismus in Deutschland. Stuttgart 1947.

PFISTER, KURT. *Deutsche Graphiker der Gegenwart.* Leipzig 1920.

GLASER, CURT. *Die Graphik der Neuzeit.* Berlin 1923.

FRIEDLÄNDER, M. J. *Die Lithographie.* Berlin 1922.

BOCK, ELFRIED. *Die Deutsche Graphik.* München 1922.

HOFFMANN, PAUL. *Ein Beitrag zur Geschichte der Lithographie.* Berlin 1924.

HÉDIARD, G. *Les Maîtres de la Lithographie.* s. d. 1893, 1901.

DUCHATEL, E. *Traité de la lithographie artistique.* Paris, s.d. (1893).

MELLERIO, A. *La Lithographie originale en couleurs.* Paris 1898.

ROSENTHAL, LÉON. *La Gravure.* Paris 1909.

DELTEIL, LOYS. *Le Peintre-Graveur Illustré,* 21 vol. Paris 1906–25.
Manuel de L'Amateur D'Estampes du XIXe et du XXe Siècle. 2 vol. texte et 2 vol. planches. Paris 1925.

ROGER MARX, CL. *La gravure originale en France de Manet à nos jours.* Paris 1939.

BERSIER, J. *La lithographie originale en France*. Paris 1943.

ADHEMAR, JEAN. *L'Estampe francaise, La Lithographie*. Paris 1944.

LANG, LÉON and J. E. BERSIER. *La lithographie en France*. I–III, Mulhouse 1946–47–52.

BÉNÉZIT, E. *Dictionnaire des Peintres, Sculpteurs, Dessinateurs et Graveurs*, 3 vol. Paris 1939. New Edition since 1948 (6 vol. published).

JOHNSON, UNA. Ambroise Vollard, Éditeur. New York 1944.

DACIER, ÉMILE. *La Gravure Francaise*. Paris 1944.

SKIRA, A. *Anthologie du Livre*. Genève 1946.
History of Modern Painting, Vol I, "from Baudelaire to Bonnard". Geneva 1949.

RIDOLFI, C. *Memoria sulla litografia, di C. R. e F. Tartini*. Firenze 1819.

OZZOLA, L. *La litografia italiana dal 1805–1870*. Roma 1923.

RATTA, C. *L'Arte della litografia in Italia*. Bologna 1930.

GOLLERBAKH, E. *History of engraving and lithography in Russia*. St Petersburg 1923 (in Russian).

PETERS, H. *America on Stone*. New York 1931.

CRAVEN, TH. *A treasury of American Prints*. New York, 1939.

THIEME, U., and BECKER, F. *Allgemeines Lexikon der bildenden Künste*, 37 vol. *bis*. 1950.

OEUVRE CATALOGUES, MONOGRAPHIES, ETC.

BARYE. L. Delteil, *Le Peintre-Graveur Illustré*, VI. Paris 1910.

BECKMANN, bei Curt Glaser u. Andere, *mit einem vollständigen Katalog von Beckmann's Graphik 1909–1923*. N.D. (1924).

BEWICK. Thomas Hugo, *The Bewick Collector*. London 1864.
Thomson, David Croal. *The Life and Works of Thomas Bewick*. London 1882.

BLAKE. Archibald, G. D. Russell, *The Engravings of William Blake*. London 1912.
Keynes, G. *William Blake's Engravings*. 1950
Gilchrist, *Life of W. Blake*. London 1863.

BOILLY. H. Harrisse, *L. L. Boilly*. Paris 1898.

BONINGTON, A. Curtis, *Catalogue de l'œuvre lithographié et gravé de R. P. Bonington*. Paris 1939.

BONNARD. Charles Terrasse, *Bonnard* (cont. l'œuvre gravé et lithogr.). Paris 1927.
Claude Roger-Marx, *Bonnard Lithographs*. Monte Carlo 1952.

BRAQUE. *Exhibition Catalogue of Das Graphische Werk Georges Braque, 1912 to the present*. Leipzig 1950.
Henry R. Hope and W. S. Lieberman, *Georges Braque*. New York 1949.

CARRIÈRE. L. Delteil, *Le Peintre-Graveur Illustré*, VIII.

CÉZANNE. L. Venturi, *Cézanne. Son Art, son Œuvre*, 2 vol. Paris 1936.

CHAGALL. *Graphic work of Marc Chagall*, part.-catalogue, Signature No. 2, New Series. London 1946.
James Johnson Sweeney, *Marc Chagall*. New York 1946.

CHARLET. La Combe, *Charlet sa vie, ses lettres* (contains catalogue of his lithographs). Paris 1856.

CHASSÉRIAU. L. Bénédite, *Chassériau, sa Vie et son Œuvre*. Paris 1931.

CORINTH. K. Schwarz, *Das graphische Werk von Lovis Corinth*. Berlin 1922.

COROT. A. Robaut, *L'Œuvre de Corot*. Paris 1905.
L. Delteil, *Le Peintre-Graveur Illustré*, V. Paris 1910.

COURBET. G. Riat, *Gustave Courbet Peintre*. Paris 1906.

DAUMIER. L. Delteil, *Le Peintre-Graveur Illustré*, XX–XXIX *bis*, 11 vol. Paris 1925–30.

DEGAS. L. Delteil, *Le Peintre-Graveur Illustré*, IX. Paris. 1919.
Denis Rouart, *Degas à la Recherche de sa Technique*. Paris 1945.

DELACROIX. L. Delteil, *Le Peintre-Graveur Illustré*, III. Paris 1908.
R. Escholier, *Delacroix, peintre, graveur, écrivain*. Paris 1926–29.

DENON. de la Fizelière, *Vivan Denon*. Paris 1883.

DEVERIA. Max Gauthier, *Achille et Eugène Deveria*. Paris 1925.

DIAZ. G. Hédiard, *N. Diaz*. Paris.

DUPRÉ. L. Delteil, *Le Peintre-Graveur Illustré*, I. Paris 1906.

ERNST. *Œuvres de Max Ernst 1919–1936*. Paris, Cahiers d'Art 1937.

FANTIN-LATOUR. G. Hédiard, *Catalogue de l'Œuvre Lithographique*. Paris 1906.

FUSELI. A. Federmann, *Heinr. Fuseli*. Zürich 1927.

GAUGUIN. M. Guérin, *L'Œuvre gravé de Gauguin*. Paris 1927.
Ch. Maurice, *Paul Gauguin*. Paris 1919.

GAVARNI. P.-A. Lemoisne, *Gavarni Peintre et Lithographe*, 2 vol. Paris 1924–8.

GÉRICAULT. L. Delteil. *Le Peintre-Graveur Illustré*, XVIII. Paris 1924.
Clément, *Géricault*. Paris 1868.

GOYA. L. Delteil. *Le Peintre-Graveur Illustré*, XIV et XV. Paris 1922.
Hofmann, F., de Goya. *Katalog seines graphischen Werkes*. Wien 1907.
Miguel Velasco Y Aguirre, *Grabados y Litografias de Goya*. Madrid 1928.

GRIS. *Sa vie, son œuvre, ses écrits;* par Henri Kahnweiler. Paris 1946. English translation, London 1947.

GROS. *Ses Amis et ses Elèves;* par R. Escholier. Paris 1936.

HUET. L. Delteil, *Le Peintre-Graveur Illustré*, VII. Paris 1911.

INGRES. L. Delteil, *Le Peintre-Graveur Illustré*, III. Paris 1908.
Vct. H. Delaborde, *Ingres, sa vie, ses travaux, sa doctrine*. Paris 1870.

ISABEY. A. Curtis, *Catalogue de l'œuvre lithographié d'Eugène Isabey*. Paris 1939.

JOHN. C. Dodgson, *Catalogue of etchings by Augustus John*. London 1920.

KANDINSKY. Will Grohmann, *Kandinsky*. Paris 1930
W. Kandinsky, *Über das Geistige in der Kunst*, München 1912.
Concerning the Spiritual in Art. London 1914; New York 1947.
Wassily Kandinsky, *Punkt und Linie zu Fläche. Bauhausbücher*, No. 9. München 1926.
Point and line to plane. New York 1946.
A catalogue of Kandinsky's Graphic work by Will Grohmann is in preparation.

KIRCHNER. Gustav Schiefler, *Die Graphik Ernst Ludwig Kirchners*. 2 vol. Berlin 1926.

KLEE. J. T. Soby, *The prints of Paul Klee*. New York 1945.
Alfred H. Barr, Feininger and Sweeney: *Paul Klee*. New York 1945.

KOKOSCHKA. Paul Westheim, *Oskar Kokoschka*. Berlin 1918.
Edith Hoffmann, *Kokoschka, Life and Work*. London 1947.
A new catalogue about the graphic work of Kokoschka, by Hans Maria Wingler is in preparation.

KOLLWITZ. Johannes Sievers, *Die Radierungen und Steindrucke von Käthe Kollwitz*. Dresden 1913.
A. Wagner, *Die Radierungen, Holzschnitte und Lithographien von Käthe Kollwitz seit 1912*. Dresden 1927.

LÉGER. Douglas Cooper, *Fernand Léger*. London and Paris-Genève 1949.
Exhibition catalogues, Tate Gallery. London 1950.

LIEBERMANN. G. Schiefler, *Das Graphische Werk von Max Liebermann*, vol. I, Berlin 1902; vol. II, Berlin 1914; and Berlin 1923.
M. Friedländer, *Max Liebermann's Graphische Kunst*. Dresden 1920.

MANET. Moreau-Nelaton, *Manet, Graveur et Lithographe*. Paris 1906.
Marcel Guérin, *L'Œuvre gravé de Manet*. Paris 1944.
Théodore Duret, *Histoire d'Edouard Manet et de son œuvre*. Paris 1902. English edition: *Manet and the French Impressionists*. London 1910.

MASSON. M. Leiris et G. Limbour, *André Masson et son Univers*. Genève-Paris 1947.

MATISSE. Alfred H. Barr, Jr, *Henri-Matisse*. New York 1951.

MENZEL. Elfried Bock, Adolf Menzel. *Verzeichnis seines graphischen Werkes*. Berlin 1923.
W. Kurth, *Adolf Menzels Graphische Kunst*. Dresden 1920.

MIRO. M. Leiris, *The prints of Joan Miro*. New York 1947.

MOORE. Herbert Read, *Henry Moore, Sculpture and Drawings*, 3rd edition. London 1949.
James J. Sweeney, *Henry Moore*. New York 1946.

MUNCH. Gustav Schiefler, *Verzeichnis des Graphischen Werkes Edv. Munch*. Vol. I *bis* 1906, Berlin 1907; Vol. II 1906–26, Berlin 1928.
G. Schiefler, "Edvard Munch's Graphische Kunst", *Arnold's Graphische Bücher*, Vol. VI. Dresden 1923.
Rolf Stenerson, *Edvard Munch*. Oslo and Zürich 1949.
Curt Glaser, *Edvard Munch*. Berlin 1918.

NASH. *Paul Nash*, edited by Margot Eates. London 1948.

NOLDE. G. Schiefler, *Das Graphische Werk von Emil Nolde*. Vol. I *bis* 1910, Berlin 1911; Vol. II 1910–25, Berlin 1926.

PICASSO. Bernhard Geiser, *Picasso peintre-graveur*. Bern 1933.
Fernant Mourlot, *Picasso lithographe*. Vol. I (1919–47); Vol. II (1947–49). Monte Carlo 1949 et 1950.
Alfred H. Barr, Jr, *Picasso, Fifty Years of his Art*. New York 1946.

PISSARRO. L. Delteil, *Le Peintre-Graveur Illustré*, XVII. Paris 1923.

PRUD'HON. Ed. de Goncourt, *Catalogue de l'œuvre peint, dessiné et gravé de P. P. Prud'hon*. Paris 1876.
J. Guiffrey, *L'Œuvre de Prud'hon*. Paris 1924.

REDON. (*Odilon*) par André Mellerio. Paris 1913.
André Mellerio, *Odilon Redon, Peintre, Dessinateur et Graveur*. Paris 1923.
Odilon Redon, *A Soi-même*. Journal (1867–1915). Paris 1922.

RENOIR. L. Delteil, *Le Peintre-Graveur Illustré*, XVIII. Paris 1923.
Cl. Roger-Marx, *les Lithographies de Renoir*. Monte Carlo 1951.

REUTER. P. Hoffmann, *Wilhelm Reuter, ein Beitrag zur Geschichte der Lithographie*. 1924.

ROUAULT. James T. Soby, *George Rouault, paintings and prints*. New York 1945.

SCHADOW. H. Mackowsky, *Schadow's Graphik*. Berlin 1936.

SCHINKEL. Dussler, *die Inkunabeln der Deutschen Lithographie*. Berlin 1928.

SIGNAC. U. Johnson, *Ambroise Vollard*. New York 1944.
Paul Signac, *D'Eugène Delacroix au Néo-Impressionisme*. Paris 1939.

SISLEY. L. Delteil, *Le Peintre-Graveur Illustré*, XVII. Paris 1923.

SLEVOGT. A. Rümann, *Verzeichnis der Graphik von Max Slevogt*. S.D. Hamburg.
E. Waldmann, *Max Slevogts graphische Kunst*. Dresden 1921.

STOTHARD. Bray, *Life of Th. Stothard*. London 1851.

SUTHERLAND. Robert Melville, *Graham Sutherland*. London 1951 and 1953.

THOMA. J. A. Beringer, *Hans Thomas Griffelkunst*. Frankfurt 1916.
J. A. Beringer, *Hans Thomas Graphik*. 1922.
H. Tannenbaum, *Hans Thomas Graphische Kunst*. Dresden 1920.

TOULOUSE-LAUTREC. L. Delteil, *Le Peintre-Graveur Illustré*, X–XI. Paris 1920.
Maurice Joyant, "Henri de Toulouse-Lautrec", *Dessins, Estampes, Affiches*, vol. II. Paris 1927.

UTRILLO. M. Gauthier, *Utrillo*. Paris 1944.

VERNET. Armand Dayot, *Les Vernet, Josef, Carle, Horace*. Paris 1898.

VILLON. (*Jacques*) *Catalogue de son œuvre gravé*, par J. Auberty et Ch. Perussaux. Paris 1950.

VUILLARD. Cl. Roger-Marx, *L'Œuvre gravé de Vuillard*. Monte Carlo 1948.

WARD. C. Reginald Grundy, *James Ward, R.A. with a Catalogue of his Engravings and Pictures*. London 1909.

WHISTLER. T. R. Way, *Whistler's Lithographs*. London 1905.

EXPLANATION OF TECHNICAL TERMS

ALGRAPHY. Process of chemical printing where aluminium sheets are used instead of stones.

AQUATINT. A process used in etching to obtain tonal effects similar to a wash, invented around 1760.

ARTIST. An artist is a painter, sculptor, engraver, etc., who expresses himself in his own original way, creating a work of art and transmitting his experience to others. The word is often misused for painter (*see* Painter).

AUTOGRAPHIE. French term for transfer lithograph.

AVANT LETTRE. *See* Before Letter.

BEFORE LETTER. A proof taken from the finished plate, before any inscription or title is added.

CATALOGUE OF PRINTS. The graphic work of most artists of the past has been catalogued and numbered so as to make it possible to identify the prints. These catalogues also contain title, date, editions and a description of the various states which exist. The prints are marked in Arabic, the states in Roman ciphers. The work of artists of the nineteenth century has mainly been catalogued by Louis Delteil, referred to as L.D.

CHALK MANNER. When lithography was invented the first artists' lithographs were all done in ink, with pen or brush. Only after stones had been grained a special chalk was used, for the first time satisfactorily in about 1804.

CHEMICAL PRINTING. Based on the antagonism of water and fat, Chemical Printing, invented by Senefelder in 1798, comprises all methods of flat printing, independent of the material used to print from. A drawing is made with a special ink or chalk, both containing certain greasy substances, on to a polished surface, stone or metal, which may have been grained beforehand. The drawing is then fixed by a solution of gum and acid. After this the plate is wetted with a sponge, the parts which have been touched by the ink or chalk reject the water. A greasy printers' ink is rolled all over the stone, the wetted parts do not accept the ink, thus only the actual design being inked, and when going through a special flat press the design appears on the paper laid over the stone or metal plate used. Chemical printing is the only method of printing from a flat surface and is completely different in principle from mechanical printing, like letterpress, wood-engraving or metal-engraving and etching.

CHROMOLITHOGRAPHY. Printing lithographs in colour from several plates, invented by Senefelder, first practised on a larger scale by Engelmann of Mulhouse.

COLOUR. The proper term for a lithograph printed from various plates in colour is "lithograph in colour" and *not* coloured lithograph, as this latter term may as well indicate a lithograph coloured by hand.

DRY STAMP. In France called *timbre sec*, used by publishers to verify the genuineness of prints.

ÉPREUVE. French term for proof.

ESTAMPE. French term for print, engraving, etching or lithograph, not made as illustration for a text.

ÉTAT. French term for state.

FLAT PRINTING PROCESS. *See* Chemical Printing.

INCUNABULA. In lithography all lithographs designed before 1817 are regarded as incunabulas. The term has been adopted from early book-printing where all books printed before 1500 are called incunabula. In Germany the year 1820 limits lithographic incunabulas.

INK. For lithography the ink must contain greasy substances. The ink can be applied with a pen or with a brush, and can be thinned out (washes).

INTAGLIO PROCESS. The lines which print are deeper than the surface of the plate and filled with ink before an impression is taken (etching, engraving, etc.).

LITHOGRAPHY. *See* Chemical Printing.

LITHOTINT. Lithotint is a method of applying washes of various densities with a brush to the stone. Invented actually by Senefelder himself, the process had its name given by Hullmandel. In France Engelmann called the method "Procédé du lavis lithographique".

ORIGINAL LITHOGRAPH. This is a lithograph drawn by the painter himself after his own design and invention. The technical process used has no bearings on the fact if a lithograph is an "original" or not, and it does not matter whether transfer-paper, stone or zinc is used. If, however, another person draws a lithograph after a painter's design, the litho is a mere reproduction, and no more an original. The same applies to colour lithographs, which can only be regarded as originals when the artist does all the necessary designs for the various colour plates himself on the plates or on transfer-paper.

PAPYROGRAPHIE. French term for lithography on stone paper.

PAPIER AUTOGRAPHIQUE. French term for transfer-paper.

PAINTER. A painter is, properly speaking, someone who knows how to handle paint and to draw.

PEINTRE-GRAVEUR. French term for a painter or sculptor who produces original graphic works.

PLATE. In lithography or chemical printing the plate can be stone, metal or a suitable substitute.

POLYAUTOGRAPHY. Name used at the beginning for chemical printing. The term was probably coined by Johannot of Offenbach, who worked in connection with the André family in Germany.

PRINT. Term used for the products of original graphic art.

PROOF. French term *épreuve*. In general, all impressions taken from a plate are called proofs. Special meanings: "trial proof" is an impression taken while the work on the plate is still in progress; "artist's proof", impressions taken for the "artist", which, as a rule, are taken before an edition is printed. (*See also* State and Before Letters.)

RELIEF PROCESS. The lines or surfaces which print are raised in comparison to the surrounding area (letterpress, woodcut, etc.).

REMARQUE. French term for a small sketch often made outside the actual area of the drawing on the plate, later removed before an edition is printed.

REPORT. French term for transfer.

SCRAPING. By this method one can make a complete drawing or take out parts of an existing drawing on the stone, for the purpose of correction or addition to the design. A lithograph done by scraping only must start on a stone, which beforehand has been blackened all over with greasy ink. Scraping can also be done on transfer-paper or metal plates, but only with limitation. Charlet did some lithographs in the scrape method.

SIGNATURE. There are two kinds of signatures: on the stone or plate itself or in pencil or ink after printing. This latter method of signing in pencil did not come into general use before about 1880. A signature in pencil is not always a guarantee of the quality of an impression, as painters did not always sign their best proofs.

SIZE. The size of a lithograph is indicated by measurements taken of the actual area covered by the drawing, including all framing lines, signature on the plate, etc., drawn by the painter on to the plate. Heights are given first. This method differs from the one used in fixing the size of etchings or engravings, where the plate-mark on the paper determines the size.

STATE. In French état. While a lithograph or engraving is in progress the painter takes some pulls in order to judge his work and to decide what alterations have to be made. These pulls taken while the work is in progress constitute the different states until the work is finished, then called final state. Further states may be created by adding a printed text or altering or omitting this again. The states before title or printer's or publisher's name are added are described as "before letters", and are of a higher intrinsical and commercial value.

STONE. The stone best suited for lithography, a porous limestone, coming from Solnhofen in Bavaria. It was used by Senefelder.

STONE PAPER. French term *carton autographique*. Invented by Senefelder, stone paper consists of sheets of carton on to which a special mixture of grained stone has been laid. The idea was to manufacture a printing surface which has the qualities of the stone without having its weight. Stone paper was used already by Géricault for a number of lithographs (*see* reproduction in Part "A").

TIMBRE SEC. French term for dry stamp.

TRANSFER-PAPER. Invented by Senefelder, transfer-paper was greatly improved about 1868. The surface of transfer-paper can be grained, like the stone. It has the great advantage that the painter can work in his studio (stones are too heavy) in just the same way as on the stone, the drawing not being made in reverse. After transfer to the stone (the whole surface of the paper with the drawing on it adheres to the stone or zinc after going several times through the lithographic press), the painter usually continues to work on it, until he obtains an impression which satisfies him. The transfer method has no influence on quality, authenticity or value of a lithograph when properly executed.

TRIAL PROOF. Impression taken while the work is in progress (*see* Proof).

ZINCOGRAPHY. Technical term for chemical printing where the plate from which the impressions are taken is made from zinc instead of stone.

INDEX

All Roman numerals refer to the text Section A, the Arabic numerals to the Illustrations and to
Section C 'Notes on Artists and their Prints'